The
Whole
Ball
of
Wax
and
Other Colloquial Phrases

The
Whole
Ball
of
Wax
and
Other Colloquial Phrases

What They Mean & How They Started

Laurence Urdang

A Perigee Book

Perigee Books
are published by
The Putnam Publishing Group
200 Madison Avenue
New York, NY 10016

Library of Congress Cataloging-in-Publication Data

Urdang, Laurence.
    The whole ball of wax and other colloquial phrases/
Laurence Urdang

        p.   cm.
    ISBN 0-399-51436-8
    Includes index
        1. English language—Provincialisms—Dictionaries.
    2. English language—Spoken English—Dictionaries.
    3. English language—Etymology—Dictionaries.
    4. English language—Terms and phrases.
    I. Title.
    PE1667.U73 1988   87-26132 CIP
    427'.09—dc19

Printed in the United States of America
1   2   3   4   5   6   7   8   9   10

For Allen Walker Read, whose career has been an inspiration to all who have followed him.

FOREWORD

An idiom is generally regarded by linguists and lexicographers as an expression that consists of two or more words with a meaning that is not readily derived from the meanings of its individual words. The term has been applied to combinations like *kick the bucket,* which has nothing to do with *kicking* or *buckets,* to *take in,* in the sense of 'deceive' *(She was easily taken in by the swindler's easy-going friendliness).* Some idioms are easy to understand, especially in context; others are quite obscure and require explanation.

Many idioms and phrases—perhaps most—are metaphors or, at least, originated as metaphors; but a metaphor is meaningful only if one is familiar with its reference, and in many instances, though the idiom has survived in the language, its metaphoric reference has fallen into disuse. For example, *kick the bucket,* an Americanism for 'die,' is said to come from a method of slaughtering hogs in which the animal was strung up on a heavy framework and its throat was cut. *Bucket* is said to be an English corruption of *buquet,* a French word for the wooden framework which the hog kicked in its death struggles. *Buquet* is not a word found in modern French dictionaries, but *boucher* 'butcher' is common enough and is, indeed, cognate with the source of English *butcher*. Yet it must be emphasized that there is no hard evidence for this etymology, in the sense that we have no valid citations for the use of French *buquet* in English. The *Oxford English Dictionary* lists *bucket* with the sense of 'beam or yoke on which anything may be hung or carried.' Though a 1597 quotation from Shakespeare that seems to carry the appropriate sense is cited, the *OED* editors were careful to state, "It is uncertain whether quot. 1597, and the proverbial phrase, relate to this word or [to *bucket* in the sense of 'pail']." The earliest given in the *OED* for *kick the bucket* is from Grose's *Dictionary of the Vulgar Tongue* (1785).

There are many such expressions in English; indeed, there are many words, which are generally easier to etymologize, for which no verifiable origins have been proven. On the other hand, some phrases that seem to have obscure histories merely refer to classical literature, the Bible, and other sources that were common knowledge among the educated and others who were contemporaneous with events of a given period. Thus, *Glaucus swap, cheveril conscience, take Hector's cloak, Judas kiss,* and many others.

In this book I have collected a number of words, phrases, and other expressions which have been selected mainly for their curiosity value, either because they have odd or interesting etymologies or because the expressions themselves reveal something useful about the way the language is used. I have deliberately omitted from consideration those expressions that seem obvious to today's readers, as well as those that may—today, at least—be regarded as clichés: *a sop to Cerberus, When in Rome . . . , quantum leap, ace in the hole, ball in one's court, through the wringer,* and similar expressions are self-evident in meaning and origin to contemporaries; whether they will remain so a hundred years hence is impossible to predict, and I shall simply have to review them then to see if they merit inclusion at the time. There has been no attempt at originality, except in their selection, for the expressions treated are well documented: where they conflict, the various experts' opinions are shown.

Also, as will be immediately apparent from the slimness of this volume, comprehensiveness, let alone completeness, is not its aim: a recent work* lists more than 250,000 individual idioms and phrases in three large volumes.

LAURENCE URDANG

OLD LYME, CONNECTICUT
1987

*Idioms & Phrases Index, Gale Research Company, 1983.

ABBREVIATIONS

DAE—Dictionary of American English
OED—Oxford English Dictionary

The
Whole
Ball
of
Wax
and
Other Colloquial Phrases

A

ABSQUATULATE
This is probably a facetious coinage, based on the *ab-* of *abscond* + *squat* + a fanciful Latin ending. It first appears in early nineteenth-century colloquial usage and means, according to an 1843 commentator, 'go and squat in another place.' Some sources define it merely as 'depart,' others add the connotation 'especially in a clandestine, surreptitious, or hurried manner.' Thus, it is equivalent to the modern Briticism, *do a moonlight flit,* often used to refer to those who leave a hotel secretly to avoid paying the bill.

AC/DC
A facetious reference to someone who is 'bisexual,' or who 'swings both ways,' this modern term plays on the common abbreviations for alternating current and direct current. It has been suggested that the abbreviation actually stands for 'anal coitus/direct coitus,' but there is no support for the conjecture, which arrived long after the expression gained currency.

ACE UP ONE'S SLEEVE
Anyone caught with any card up his sleeve in a gambling context would be assumed to be cheating. It is curious, then, to note that this expression, a common Americanism, has come to mean to 'hold something useful, powerful, or valuable in reserve,' without any suggestion of dishonesty.

ALL TALK AND NO CIDER

An American expression meaning 'a lot of hot air and no action.' The proverb was first recorded by Washington Irving in *Salmagundi* (1807) and could be taken as encouragement for "more cider and less talk"—especially if it was hard cider.

ALMIGHTY DOLLAR

In 1837, Washington Irving wrote, in *The Magnolia,* "The almighty dollar, that great object of universal devotion throughout our land. . . . I . . . prayed that the inhabitants might long retain their happy ignorance . . . and their contempt for the almighty dollar." In 1855, according to the *DAE,* Irving claimed that the phrase was "used for the first time in this sketch." But the *DAE* shows a citation from 1836: "(Phila.) Public Ledger, 2 Dec. 'The Almighty Dollar' is the only object of worship." As the phrase is usually attributed to Irving, this evidence would appear to confute his claim.

ALUMNUS, ALUMNI, ALUMNA, ALUMNAE

Although the words *alumnus* and *alumna* (and their plurals, *alumni* and *alumnae*) seem to have acquired the patina of an age-long presence in English, the first citation shown for *alumnus* in the *OED* is only from *Evelyn's Diary* (written in 1645, published 1827). Moreover, it occurred only rarely before it was picked up by Americans and legitimized by continual usage from 1696 onward. At the time the *OED* entry was published (1888), the word was still regarded as unassimilated in the language. Its origin is in Latin *alumnus* 'foster child,' which gives some indication of how educational institutions in America felt about their graduates. The first citation for the feminine form, *alumna,* is shown in the *DAE* as 1882. As this postdated the probable date of preparation of the *OED* entry, it is understandable that the *OED* shows no listing for *alumna* till the publication of the Supplement (1933).

AMERICANISM

DAE: 'A word, phrase, or idiom peculiar to American usage in speech or writing, as contrasted with that of England or other English-speaking countries.' According to the citation given, the term was coined by Witherspoon, an American, in writings that appeared in 1781 (published in England in 1794).

AMY DARDIN'S HORSE

This metaphor for 'delay, procrastination,' especially in expected action by a government, gained currency in the two decades beginning in 1796 during which Amy Dardin, a widow of Mecklenburg County, Virginia, pursued her protracted claim for compensation by the U.S. government for the loss of a horse, the exact circumstances of which are not known.

ANNIE OAKLEY

Annie Oakley (1860–1926) was a real person, a renowned trickshot expert who entertained with Buffalo Bill's Wild West Show. One of her famous tricks was to shoot the pips from a playing card that had been tossed into the air. As the perforated card bore a resemblance to an admission ticket that had been punched on presentation, *Annie Oakley* was applied to the latter and, by the magic of transferred meaning, became an informal synonym for a 'free pass.' The term has lost much of its popularity with the passage of time and is not so frequently used today; yet it is still recognized and has been enshrined in the literature of America from the early twentieth century.

ANTIFOGMATIC

Any spirituous beverage, as whisky, rum, etc., taken to ward off the effects of fog, especially the morning fog that results from overimbibing of the cure the evening before. The first citation shown in the *DAE* is for 1789. A variant (1828) is *fogmatic.*

ARKANSAS TOOTHPICK
A large **bowie knife** (*q.v.*), especially one in which the hinged blade could be folded into the handle (1837). Also called **California toothpick.**

ASPHALT JUNGLE
An Americanism, a cynical metaphor for a city viewed as a hard place where the law of the jungle—survival of the fittest, dog-eat-dog—prevails. Though this is a modern, early twentieth-century term, it is interesting to note that the word *asphalt* has been used in English from at least the fourteenth century and that it appears in the Bible (in Greek) in the sense 'slime,' according to the *OED*. Its universal, unspecialized reference has always been to some sort of black, bituminous substance. *The Asphalt Jungle* was the title of a movie (1950) starring Louis Calhern and Sterling Hayden, and featuring a newcomer to films, Marilyn Monroe. The term *jungle* applied metaphorically to a city in the sense of 'savage' appears early in the twentieth century but gained wide currency after publication (1906) of *The Jungle* by Upton Sinclair, an exposé of the meat-packing industry in Chicago that led to many labor reforms.

ASSASSIN COLLAR
A high, stiff man's collar in the style worn from the middle 1800s, so called because its edge was rather sharp against the neck.

AT LOGGERHEADS
'In dispute' is the gloss of this common expression. According to the *Century Dictionary*, the semantics of the word *log* ('trimmed trunk of a tree') originated with the notion of 'thick'; thus, we have *logy* 'slow, stupid' from *loggy* 'like a log.' A *loggerhead* was a 'dunce or slow-witted fool.' Hence, *at loggerheads* became 'bickering and arguing like fools, especially about trifling matters.' The *OED* derives the idiom from a specialized sense of *loggerhead* as a 'spherical mass of iron with a long handle, heated and used, e.g., to liquefy tar,' the suggestion being that the instru-

ment might have been used as a weapon. There is little evidence, however, that such loggerheads were used as weapons with sufficient frequency to have given rise to an idiom—certainly, loggerheads were likely to have been rarer than, say, axes, spades, or other utensils easily used as weapons—and the *Century* analysis seems the more sensible.

AT SIXES AND SEVENS

This common idiom, meaning 'in a disordered or confused state,' has a very long history in the language; yet, for all that, its origin is obscure, though theories abound. The one most often quoted is in the *OED,* which offers *set on cinque and sice* ('five and six') as the original form, which suggests the hazards of dice (if that is not redundant). That is fine as far as it goes and makes even more sense if one accepts a previous meaning of 'chancy.' But the shift from 'chancy' to 'confused' is a very great semantic leap. Moreover, there is no explanation of the transition from *on cinque and sice* to *at six and seven* to *at sixes and sevens,* nor is there any evidence of a transitional form. To complicate matters further, one early form is *at six and sevens,* which might give rise to the hypothesis that *six* is a spelling form for *sics;* obsolete *sic* in many of its uses meant 'such,' but it was also used in numerical expressions. So *by sic seven (be sic sevin)* is described in the *OED* as a comparison meaning 'seven times more, better, etc.' This usage is far from self-evident to the speaker of Modern English and, at any rate, yields little insight into the development of *at sixes and sevens.* Yet another theory suggests that the phrase arose because of a persistent dispute concerning which of two semi-officials should follow sixth or seventh in the king's retinue. While this seems as implausible as all the others, it is, on the other hand, just as likely till the gaps in the evidence have been filled by some as-yet-unattested source.

ATTACK OF THE SLOWS

Racetrack slang for the affliction suffered by a horse that does not cover the distance quickly enough to finish **in the money** (*q.v.*).

B

BALL OF WAX

Often extended to *whole ball of wax,* this idiom has puzzled etymologists, though its semantic origins seem obvious enough: wax is not only a substance to which almost anything will stick but also a material which will retain the impression of anything that comes in contact with it. The reference is to ordinary wax, like beeswax, not to 'hard wax,' like sealing wax, which consists largely of lacquer. From these literal beginnings, it is not hard to understand the metaphoric extensions the phrase has undergone to its present-day meaning of 'all things included.' It is frequently used as an adjective, as in a *ball-of-wax price,* a price that includes everything, e.g., costs of materials, installation, taxes, and so forth. There is no evidence found for its use outside of American English.

BALLPARK FIGURE

This recent (post-World War II) phrase is obviously an Americanism: no other English-speaking country conducts sports in ballparks, in which the reference is to baseball.

It means a 'reasonable estimate.' One might say in nego-
tiating the price of almost anything, "I realize that you
cannot give me an exact quotation but let me have a ballpark figure." The phrase was probably transferred from
out of the ballpark, meaning 'completely out of my range;
entirely unrealistic.' The literal origin is obvious to those
familiar with baseball: *out of the ballpark* is 'totally out of
reach; not negotiable,' since a (fair) ball hit "over the fence"
is not playable and constitutes an automatic home run. Its
variants frequently appear: *in the (right) ballpark; not in* or
out of the ballpark, etc. *Ballpark* is used frequently today in
England and, perhaps, in other countries where Americans
conduct business and English is spoken.

BARK UP THE WRONG TREE

The figurative meaning of this expression, 'be in error
about one's suspicions, follow a wrong trail,' according to
the evidence available, is virtually contemporaneous with
its literal uses, referring to a dog's barking at a tree that
does not contain the raccoon, opossum, or other animal
being chased. Two early quotations (1833 and 1834) record
its uses by Davy Crockett, later hero of the Alamo.

(LIKE A) BAT OUT OF HELL

The common speculation about the origin of this expression is that it is (first) an Americanism and (second) somehow related to the aversion that the small, winged mammal
has to light "and especially to the illumination from the
fires of hell." As far as the second part is concerned, there
is no evidence that bats have an aversion to light: because
of their built-in "radar" they do not require light to nav-
igate and find food. There is an old—in fact, obsolete—
word *batte* 'rush, hurry.' At least one commentator has
related it to the word *bat,* unrelated to the animal bat, from
which the word for 'cudgel, (cricket) bat, (baseball) bat,
etc.' comes. The *OED* shows several nineteenth-century
citations for this *bat* meaning 'beat; rate of stroke or speed;
pace,' among them, from 1880: "Going off at a lively bat
of 34 . . . the boat travelled at good pace." Once the sense

of 'speed' had disappeared from the language, it is not untoward to assume that *bat,* which was slang to begin with and might well have been used with other reinforcing words for which written records are lacking, was consistently reinforced by "out of hell." If this assumption is correct, then the first speculation, that the phrase is an Americanism, is no longer supportable, for the citations in the *OED* are all from English and Scottish sources, and there are no American citations given in the *Century* or other older dictionaries of American English.

BEAT GENERATION

An Americanism, coined by poet and novelist Jack Kerouac in the 1950s to describe the "lost generation" of World War II, who rejected the standards of contemporary society and demonstrated their rebellious attitude by outlandish dress and behavior. The term, according to personal correspondence with Kerouac, came from *beatitude,* but that may be taken with a grain of salt. In any event, it was popularized by him and by his associates, Allen Ginsberg and, especially, Lawrence Ferlinghetti, who published much of the writing of the set and offered it through his San Francisco bookshop, City Lights, which was a focal point of readings and other "beatnik" activities. *Beatnik* was coined later and came to refer to anyone who dressed unconventionally, wore a beard and his hair long, and generally looked like a slob. The Liverpudlian musical group of fame probably called themselves *Beatles* partly in admiration of the American beatniks, partly as a punning reference to beetles. Unlike their namesakes, who certainly looked as if they were impecunious, the Beatles, as is well known, did not take a vow of poverty.

BEAT THE DONICKER

Donicker is an old Americanism for 'toilet,' usually in reference to a public toilet: *donicker hustlers* or *workers* are petty thieves who rob patrons of public restrooms. Its origin is unknown. *Beat the donicker* means to 'hide in the restroom of a train car to avoid being asked for a ticket by the trainman.' It is an old ruse that rarely works on American trains today, now that ticket stubs or receipts must be displayed.

BEAT THE RAP

It is likely that this slang Americanism originated in another expression, *take the rap,* in which *rap* is slang for 'punishment,' facetiously, from a "rap on the knuckles." One who takes the rap for someone else stands in for the other's punishment. *Beat the rap* means 'avoid suffering the punishment for a wrongdoing,' and it often carries with it the connotation that the miscreant was actually guilty, though acquitted. Rap has also acquired the transferred meaning 'accusation for a crime,' especially in the noun phrase *bum rap,* a 'false accusation or indictment, frame-up.'

BEE: SEWING-BEE, SPELLING-BEE, HUSKING-BEE, ETC.

The earliest evidence for *bee* in the sense of 'a gathering of neighbors to accomplish something together' is from the mid seventeenth century. The word has been used in a wide variety of combinations with terms denoting some activity, as, in addition to those shown above, *quilting, logging, spinning,* and so on. The *DAE* maintains that there is no evidence for the statement offered by the *OED* to the effect that the use of *bee* in these contexts is in allusion to the social and industrious behavior of that insect.

BEECHER'S BIBLE

An obsolete sardonic metaphor for the Sharp rifle, in allusion to Henry Ward Beecher's comment, published in the *New York Evening Post* in February 1856, that "the Sharp rifle was a truly moral agency, . . . [with] more moral power . . . , so far as the slaveholders of Kansas were concerned, than a hundred Bibles."

BEELINE
The straight or shortest route followed by a bee in returning to its hive from gathering honey (1830).

BEER GARDEN
An outdoor area, usually attached to an inn, tavern, or other drinking establishment, that is equipped with tables and chairs for customers who frequent the place to drink beer. It is a loanword from German *Biergarten* (1870).

BE LEFT HOLDING THE BAG or BABY
The American expression is more commonly . . . *holding the bag,* the British, . . . *holding the baby.* Both mean to 'have been given the blame or responsibility for something either through inadvertence or by having been made a fool of by someone who decamps.' The American form may come from the old confidence trick known as the **drop game** (*q.v.*) in which the sucker is left holding a (hand)bag filled with worthless paper. The more humorous British version is based on the incident in which a traveler at a train station is asked by a young woman if he will hold her baby while she attends to some brief errand, like buying a ticket. She disappears into the crowd and he, poor fellow, is left holding the baby. An earlier version of the American variant is *to leave* or *give one the bag to hold* or *leave in the lurch.* It is noteworthy that what is today the more common American (. . . *bag)* version was originally British, with a citation in the *OED* for 1592, and that the current British (. . . *baby)* version, according to evidence cited in the *OED,* was originally American, the earliest quotation going back to 1927.

BETWEEN A ROCK AND A HARD PLACE
Meaning 'in a predicament, forced to choose between two equally undesirable or possibly fatal alternatives,' this modern American cliché seems to be a paraphrase of the classical expression *between Scylla and Charybdis:* indeed, Scylla was

a huge rock, a danger to navigation, in the Strait of Messina, between Italy and Sicily; Charybdis was an equally perilous whirlpool nearby. In the *Odyssey,* Odysseus was compelled to sail the treacherous waters between them, Scylla being personified as a sea monster, and lost both ship and crew, barely surviving himself. It is conjectured that while Scylla remained the *rock,* Charybdis, a difficult word to pronounce and remember, might have become the *hard place,* partly for simplification, partly in an access of scornful denigration of the classical referent as too highbrow. Curiously, *between a rock and a whirlpool* is not found. See also **between the devil and the deep blue sea.**

BETWEEN THE DEVIL AND THE DEEP BLUE SEA

Research reveals a single source, cited in the *OED,* for *devil* in the sense 'seam in the bottom of a (wooden) ship at the waterline.' Without corroborative evidence, *Funk & Wagnalls Dictionary* defines *devil* as the 'seam between the garboard strake and the keel.' Those familiar with wooden sailing vessels know that the seam at the garboard strake (the plank alongside the keel) is critical to the watertight integrity of the hull; between the normal working of the hull in bad weather and the enormous strains placed on the keel, coupled with the fact that a rigid lead keel can often separate from the contiguous wooden members owing to differences in expansion and contraction, the garboard seams of a vessel can be quite sensitive to opening, clearly an undesirable occurrence. All of this makes good sense, and it is from such feasibility that folk etymology is born. The difficulty in treating the etymology with much credibility lies in the lack of supporting evidence for this sense of *devil:* all wooden ships for centuries had (sensitive) garboard seams, and it seems very unlikely, were *devil* habitually so used, that evidence for it would crop up in only one source. Rather, it is far more likely that the expression, which means 'caught between two equally undesirable choices,' is semiliteral, that is, 'caught between dealing with the dangers of his satanic majesty and those of Davy Jones's locker.' See also **the devil to pay (and no pitch hot)** and **between a rock and a hard place.**

BEYOND THE PALE
Pale is not a common word any longer except in this cliché, but it is cognate with *palisade,* a 'fence made of stakes driven into the ground vertically side by side.' It originally referred to the fence or paling that marked off the area of jurisdiction of some sort of authority: hence, anything outside or beyond the pale was "outside the jurisdiction of" that authority.

BILLINGSGATE
This relic from older London days is still used to denote 'foul, obscene language.' It is named for the fish market, formerly at Billingsgate in London, and for the boisterous, foulmouthed porters and fishwives who bickered their way through the early-morning hours there, noisily screaming and arguing over their noisome merchandise.

BITE THE BULLET
This was probably a military expression literally stemming from the practice of giving a wounded soldier a lead bullet to clench his teeth on to help him strain against the pain of field surgery without the benefit of an anesthetic. Once anesthetics became available, the idiom became metaphoric. It is used figuratively today to mean to 'persevere, come what may.'

BLACKBERRY WINTER
In rural areas of the United States the weather is as much a topic of conversation as in the urban areas—and, indeed, in London, Paris, and everywhere else; though perhaps the designations are a bit more colorful. A *blackberry winter* is a cold spell that occurs after the blackberries have started to bloom, in late May or early June. On this formula, there are many such expressions:

blackbird storm: a cold spell after the blackbirds have returned (late spring).

buzzard storm: a cold spell after the buzzards have returned (late spring).

dogwood winter: a cold spell after the dogwood has begun to bloom in late spring.

frog storm: a period of bad weather in the spring after a spell of fine weather.

martin storm: a blizzard in the spring, after the martins have returned.

oak winter: a cold spell after the oak leaves have appeared in the spring.

whippoorwill storm: a cold storm in late spring, when whippoorwills call.

BLAZE A TRAIL

In the sense of 'white spot on the face of a horse or ox,' *blaze* is attested in England as early as 1639 (*OED*). But its transferred meaning, 'a light patch left on a tree after stripping off a piece of bark,' is an Americanism dating to 1662 *(DAE)*. The verb phrase, *blaze a trail* 'mark a trail with blazes,' shows evidence of use as early as 1750 in the literal sense, but citations for the contemporary figurative use, 'mark a way for others to follow,' have not been found antedating 1850.

BLIND PIG

'A place where illicit liquor is sold.' A variant is *blind tiger*. Both date to the late nineteenth century. Why "blind"? The *OED Supplement* is silent on the meaning of *blind* that might apply, but the *DAE* suggests, "From the professed

object of exhibition." This explanation is obscure: does it mean that operators of such establishments actually exhibited blind pigs? That seems unlikely, to be sure. More probable is the notion that "blind" in *blind pig* and *blind tiger* referred to their having no windows.

BLUE CHIPS

Today, these are the stock market shares of major, solvent, successful corporations that form secure investments. By transference, those corporations themselves are often termed the *blue chips:* "The blue chips advanced on the Market today." The tokens used in betting at poker are called *chips* and come in white, red, and blue, in order of increasing value. The adoption by the stock-exchange gamblers of the poker-table gamblers is patent. To *cash in one's chips* means to 'trade one's chips for money' when one leaves a game of poker; metaphorically, it has come to mean to 'depart the game of life,' that is, to 'die.' *Checks* is another, older word for chips in poker, and one who ceases play *checks out,* which can now be done at hotels (after one has *checked in*).

BLUE LAWS

A set of strictly puritanical regulations promulgated in the seventeenth and eighteenth centuries in the New Haven (Connecticut) colony. Their name is said to derive from their being printed on blue paper. They were later extended to other areas within the state. For the most part, the term was originally applied to stringent measures against breaking the sabbath on the principle, as described by Thomas Jefferson, "that the laws of God shall be the laws of their land." It was reported that some were so severe as to include the death penalty for any clergyman of the Church of England (which was outlawed) who might be found within the state. Most of the laws were repealed or, at least, went unenforced well into the nineteenth century. But as recently as the 1980s some were revived to enjoin designated businesses from operating on Sundays, partly on the grounds that employees of those establishments might be exploited, partly because certain religious factions maintain influence in the state legislature. Although no longer rigorously enforced, such laws remain on the books of New England states other than those of Connecticut.

BLUE-SKY LAWS
These should be distinguished from **blue laws** *(q.v.)*, which are a reflex of zealous Puritanism. *Blue-sky laws* were those enacted originally in Kansas, in 1911, and later adopted by other states, aimed at controlling the sale of fraudulent stocks and bonds. According to a news item of the day, they received their name because the high-flown plans of ambitious promoters virtually sought to capitalize the "blue skies."

BOARDINGHOUSE DECEIVER
A suitcase—usually a cheap one—left in a hotel room to delude the chambermaid into thinking that the tenant is remaining another day, when, in fact, he has **absquatulated** *(q.v.)*.

BOOTLEGGER
Bootleggers were so named because they concealed their illegal liquor in their bootlegs—that is, literally, the legs of their boots. When one considers the vast quantities of illicit booze moved about the American countryside during Prohibition, such quantities as could be literally bootlegged seems so small—in comparison with the true volume of illicit traffic—as to have been scarcely worth the effort.

BOOTLICKING

Although this word and its other forms—*bootlick, boot-licker*—seem British in origin, they appear to be Americanisms for 'toadying, brown-nosing sycophancy' and date from about the middle of the nineteenth century. See also **toady**.

BORSCHT BELT or CIRCUIT

Borscht (properly *borshcht*) is soup made from beef stock and red beets; it is eaten hot or cold, but usually cold, with pieces of boiled potato and a dab of sour cream. Essentially a Polish-Russian dish, it was very popular with the Jews from eastern Europe who immigrated to the United States from the late nineteenth century onward. Many of them settled in New York City and, after they became well enough established to be able to afford vacations, found the nearby Catskill Mountains, north of the city, much to their liking. Enterprising hoteliers built resorts there, offering all sorts of opportunities for sport and recreation. In addition, they soon engaged singers, comedians, and other performers to entertain guests in the evenings. Many of these would be booked into one resort after another, making a tour throughout the region. The tour came to be called the *Borscht Circuit* and the area in which the resorts were—and still are—situated, the *Borscht Belt*. The hotels also employ *tummelers,* people (usually men) whose function it is to generate activities among the guests by playing games, engaging in charades, and so on. The origin of *tummeler* is vague; but while speculation has it that it comes from *tumult,* which is what a tummeler is hired to create, it is more likely to have its origins in Yiddish, going back

to German *tummeln* 'romp' and *Tummelplatz* 'playground.'
See also **strawhat circuit.**

BOSS

This word, so widely used in all forms of English today,
originated in Dutch *baas* 'master, foreman' when it was
borrowed into American English at the beginning of the
nineteenth century. The first citation in the *DAE* is from
1806. Its use as a verb is not attested till fifty years later,
shortly followed by *bossism*. Its adjectival sense, 'groovy,'
did not appear till another hundred years had passed.

BOWERY BOY

One of a set of tough rowdies who frequented the Bowery,
in New York City. In the eighteenth century, the Bowery,
on the site of the former country seat of that name owned
by Governor Peter Stuyvesant, became a tree-lined bou-
levard on the Lower East Side of Manhattan, frequented
by—what else?—the boulevardiers of the day. By the early
1800s it had been overtaken by the expanding city and
began to be frequented by those who preyed on the better
class of people, who soon abandoned the place. In the 1840s
a contemporary referred to the *round rimmers* ". . . in New
York, a name applied to a large class of dissipated young
men, by others called Bowery boys. . . ." Although today
the Third Avenue Elevated Railway has long since gone
on the scrap-heap, the Bowery remains the characteristic
skid row (*q.v.*) of New York, populated by tramps, drunks,
and other down-and-outers who, for a handout, offer to
wipe off the windshields of those motorists unlucky enough
to be caught there at a traffic light.

BOWIE KNIFE

A heavy, double-edged sheath knife, about twelve inches
long, with a curved blade and a sharp point, said to have
been fashioned from a broken sword by Colonel James
Bowie, who was killed at the Battle of the Alamo, March
6, 1836. The *DAE* cites part of a letter from a Rezin P.
Bowie in *Niles' Register* in which he wrote (1838), "The

first Bowie knife was made by myself." Research has yielded nothing about R. P. Bowie or his claim. See also **Arkansas toothpick**.

BRAINSTORM

The modern sense of this word is a 'brilliant idea' or, as a verb, to 'solve a problem or seek to develop imaginative ideas by active exchange among a small group.' The older sense referred to a severe mental condition, what might today be termed 'temporary insanity.' In 1906, Harry K. Thaw was tried for shooting to death the famous architect Stanford White at the Roof Garden of the old Madison Square Garden in New York City, for carrying on a liaison with his wife, Evelyn Nesbit, the actress known as the "Girl in the Red Velvet Swing." Thaw's lawyer pleaded not guilty on behalf of his client on the grounds that he had suffered a brainstorm. He lost.

BROWNED OFF

Partridge reports that this slang expression had its origins in sodomy, which seems as unlikely (whence the sense of 'incensed, furious'?) as his tracing it to *brassed off,* having to do with brass buttons tarnishing to dark brown: neither yields the appropriate semantic connection. Everyone knows the expression *pissed off,* a somewhat milder version of the same term. If *pissed off* 'angry' comes from the notion that the individual so afflicted is angry enough to lose control and urinate in his pants, then *browned off* might well be an intensification of such fury that would cause a person to defecate in his pants.

BUCKET SHOP

This nineteenth-century New York term for an 'office dealing in penny shares or shares in lots of one or five at a time' has been metaphorically extended to include 'any business of questionable integrity that offers services at prices below those of the competition.' It need not be a dealer in stocks and bonds: in recent years discount travel agencies have been called *bucket shops*. Because many such businesses operate on a very narrow margin of profit and are consequently often in a precarious condition, their customers occasionally lose money in them, adding to their disrepute. The original bucket shops were unlicensed liquor dispensaries—gin mills, or **blind tigers** (*q.v*)—that sold spirits illegally in pitchers or, literally, in buckets. See also **blind pig**.

BUG JUICE
In British English this term, according to Partridge, has become specialized in the sense of 'any alcoholic beverage.' In American English, it remains schoolboy slang, heard especially in summer camps, used to refer to any beverage with unidentifiable ingredients, though always a soft drink, often just water with sugar, fruit juice, and, sometimes, a vegetable coloring. Some report it means, almost literally, 'insect repellent.'

BULLS AND BEARS
A folk etymology is a plausible, though inaccurate, tale recounting the origin of a word or phrase. A frequently encountered etymology for the term *bull and bear* in stock exchange parlance is that the *bulls* are so called because they come charging out brashly into the arena, full of aggression; *bears,* on the other hand, are said to be somewhat more cautious and retiring, avoiding conflict, and hibernating. Although the evidence for the origin of the stock-market *bull* is vague and inconclusive, *bear* is well documented: an eighteenth-century dictionary lists the phrase *sell a bear,* meaning to 'sell something one does not own.' It is apparently the remnant of an old proverb, *sell the bearskin before catching the bear.* In London's Exchange

Alley, where the business of buying and selling shares began, a *bearskin* was the name given to shares sold by a speculator who did not own them on the expectation that their price would go down. Such a speculator was termed a *bearskin jobber,* later shortened to *bear. Bull* is of about the same vintage; it might have become connected with bear through the association in people's minds between *bearbaiting* and *bullbaiting,* popular "sports" of the day.

BUNK

This word for 'claptrap, nonsense, humbug' has been thoroughly documented as arising from an episode that took place in 1819, during the Sixteenth Congress. A long-winded congressman from North Carolina, F. Walker, was advised to discontinue his tiresome speech as the other members were all leaving, to which he is reported to have replied, "Never mind; I'm talking to Buncombe," the name of the county of his constituency. The early uses of the allusion, in which, incidentally, the word appeared as *bunkum,* seem to have been applied specifically to empty political talk (1828): *Niles' Register* of that year refers to *talking to Bunkum* as "an old and common saying at Washington," which seems to indicate that in order to be regarded as "old" after only ten years it must by that time have already become a cliché. Although the forms *bunkum* and *buncome* vied for popularity during the nineteenth century, the modern form is almost always *bunk,* sometimes *bunkum.* This *bunk* is not related at all to the *bunk* meaning a certain kind of bed. Though most sources give as the etymology of *bunco* 'swindle' the Spanish *banca* 'a card-game resembling monte,' it seems likely, even if such is the case, that *bunco* and its various compounds—*bunco-steerer, bunco artist, bunco squad, buncoist,* etc.—which appeared later on in the 1800s, were at least influenced by *bunkum.*

BURY THE HATCHET

An American Indian warrior carried a tomahawk, a kind of hatchet, as a weapon. If peace broke out, the opposing sides would *bury the hatchet* as a symbol of the cessation of hostilities. (The phrase does not, as some would have it, mean to "bury the hatchet in someone's head.") *Bury the hatchet* conveys the sense of a mutual agreement. Thus, it is today confined mainly to personal feuds rather than major conflicts, which are settled by unconditional surrender or, as in the case of the Vietnam war, unconditional withdrawal.

C

CALIFORNIA BANK NOTE
An animal hide regarded as a legitimate medium of exchange, so called by sailors according to Richard Henry Dana's *Two Years Before the Mast* (1840).

CALIFORNIA PRAYER BOOK
A facetious term for a 'pack of cards,' dating from the mid nineteenth century.

CALIFORNIA TOOTHPICK
A **Bowie knife** (*q.v.*) See also **Arkansas toothpick.**

CALIFORNIA WIDOW
A woman whose husband deserted her for a long period to seek his fortune in California during the Gold Rush, 1850–60. This sense of *widow* ('any woman left alone while her husband was off engaging in some activity') has become productive in English, and we now have *golf widows, fishing widows, computer widows,* etc. Those instances in which the husband has been left behind while his wife pursues

her interests has not resulted in the substitution "widower," and men are facetiously referred to as *widows* in such contexts. See also **grass widow.**

CALLITHUMPIAN BAND
An informal musical band in which the instruments consist of bells, rattles, tin pans, and the like, characteristically producing discordant music. The term, which also appears in the noun form *callithump,* goes back to the 1840s and is of unknown or "fanciful" origin, according to the sources.

CANNON BROAD
A 'proficient female pickpocket.' The *broad* is obvious; the *cannon,* according to Maurer, is derived ultimately from Yiddish *gonif, gonef,* or *ganef* 'thief,' which yielded *gun,* which yielded *cannon.* However, *gun* yields *cannon* directly, and the sinuous derivation would seem unnecessary—except for the fact that pickpockets rarely, if ever, carry guns. Thus, *cannon* is best described as from *ganef* and therefore means 'thief,' not 'gun.' It also occurs in *class cannon* 'adroit pickpocket,' especially one who, according to Maurer, "observes the professional code of ethics," and in *live cannon,* 'a pickpocket who robs a "moving" victim,' as a purse snatcher, in contrast with a *lush buster,* 'one who robs, or rolls, drunks.' A *solo* or *single-o cannon* is a 'pickpocket who prefers to work alone.' A *summer cannon* is 'one who is unable to rob a victim who is wearing a coat and therefore moves to the sunbelt for the winter season of filchery.'

CAPE ANN TURKEY
See **Cape Cod turkey.**

CAPE COD TURKEY
A facetious name for 'salted codfish.' It was first documented in this form in 1865, apparently replacing the earlier *Cape Ann turkey* (1844), which meant the same thing. Also called **Marblehead turkey.**

CAPE MAY DIAMOND

A jocular name for a 'paste gem', so named (1866) in reference to Cape May, the southernmost point of New Jersey, where those who frequented the cheap resorts were not able to afford the real thing. Another theory holds that Cape May was the site of a number of nudist colonies, where the wearing of genuine gems was ill-advised.

CARPETBAGGER

This common Americanism is well known in the sense of a 'person who descends on others in order to exploit them when they are at some disadvantage.' Many Americans who recall their history lessons remember that it was the name given to those Northerners who went south during the Reconstruction, at the end of the War Between the States when the South was in **shambles** (*q.v.*), to cheat and swindle the people out of the little they had left. In those lessons pupils were told that the reason these unscrupulous louts were called *carpetbaggers* was that they carried carpet bags—that is, satchels made from carpeting material. A properly inquiring mind might have wondered why these fellows so conveniently outfitted themselves uniformly, which would surely have made them easy to identify and thus avoid. The answer lies in the fact that carpet bags were merely the popular carry-alls of the day, not quite the same as today's shopping bags, but far less costly than leather or fitted suitcases, which only the wealthy could afford. Besides, carpet bags were quite commodious, allowing the raider to carry with him all his worldly possessions. The application of the term *carpetbagger* to an "unscrupulous exploiter" goes back to an earlier period when speculating bankers invaded the West, took advantage of the early settlers, and absconded with the bank's funds in innocent-looking carpet bags.

CARRY (SOMEONE) ON A CHIP

An Ozark Mountain idiom meaning to 'spoil, pamper.'

CARRY THE TORCH FOR (SOMEONE)

The prevailing theories of the source of this American idiom agree that it has its origins in the American practice of lending support to a political candidate by (literally) carrying a torch in a campaign parade. 'Lend support to' easily shifted over to 'be devoted to,' and its subsequent modern reflex, 'be so much in love with someone that any diversion of interest is out of the question.' Although the expression is used to refer to lovers of either sex, its secondary derivatives, *torch song* and *torch singer*, refer to melodies and performers associated only with women—women who are suffering the blues because their love is impossible (for any number of reasons) or unrequited.

CATCH-22

It is not often (as can be seen from some of the other entries in this book) that the origin of an expression can be pinpointed with precision, but *catch-22* illustrates one of those rare occurrences: Joseph Heller's novel, *Catch-22*, was published in 1961, and about a dozen years later its title had become an idiom in the language (among those who could not abide its low synonym, a 'no-win situation'). The title and idiom refer to a feature of the book's plot, which takes place during World War II. It concerns pilots at an airbase who are required to fly far more missions than they can endure: the strain tells on them, and they try to do anything to be relieved of duty. Fatigue and exhaustion are not sufficient cause for furlough because of the pressures of the day. The only valid grounds for relief from duty are insanity or, of course, death in combat. If a pilot applies for leave to avoid combat, he is deemed sane, hence cannot be relieved on the grounds of insanity. Thus, he is in an inescapable trap, or a *catch-22*. It is a discouraging thought, but one is given to wonder if some etymologist, a few hundred years from now, finding this documentation for the origin of the expression will not decide its explanation improbable, reject it, and substitute some fancied folk etymology for the true one.

CATHOLIC ASPIRIN
A slang term used by narcotics addicts for an 'amphetamine,' so called because it has score marks in the shape of a cross on each tablet.

(LIKE A) CAT IN A STRANGE GARRET
An expression describing someone who is overly timid, amazed, or frightened (1824).

CHINESE NEEDLEPOINT or NEEDLEWORK
A euphemistic expression used by narcotics addicts to refer to 'dealing in or using narcotics, especially opium.' Maurer shows a citation, "He has a store in Frisco, now, sells jewelry and novelties and Chinese needlework."

(CARRY, HAVE, GO ABOUT WITH, etc.) A CHIP ON ONE'S SHOULDER
An Americanism meaning to 'display aggressiveness, spoil for a fight.' Its literal origins seem to have been in the Midwest, the earliest citation given in the *DAE* being from a St. Louis newspaper of 1840. The sought-after combatant was said to knock a chip from (or off) someone's shoulder. A hint of its original sense might be seen in a quotation

from *Harper's* magazine (1857) in which "shoulder-hitters" are referred to. Is it possible that this suggests that many fights were started deliberately (or inadvertently) by one man giving another a shove in the shoulder?

(LEAD-PIPE) CINCH

'Anything done easily or with a minimum of effort.' This nineteenth-century Americanism is traced to *cinch*, meaning a 'saddle girth,' a word borrowed from Mexican Spanish. For even the slightest security a cinch must hold fast, and the word came to be used to mean a 'sure thing,' then 'something easily accomplished.' The question of where the modifier *lead-pipe* came from is not so clear: it might have been added merely as an intensifier, but why it is "lead-pipe," which appeared around the beginning of the twentieth century, has not been satisfactorily explained.

CLEAN (SOMEONE'S) PLOW

To 'deliver a sound thrashing' to someone; to 'beat up badly.' The Ozark farmer cleans his plow of rust and dirt by driving it through abrasive gravel or coarse sand. Randolph and Wilson report that a more primitive type may well utter the threat, "I'm gonna clean that man's plow," and that after a fight backwoodsmen appear very much the worse for wear and tear (though not less dirty).

COLD TURKEY

This phrase has lately come to describe any sudden withdrawal from a habit like smoking or the eating of chocolate. It is used adverbially, as in *I quit cold turkey,* or as an adjective, *I took a cold-turkey cure.* Its origins are in the description of one of the symptoms seen in a person who is abruptly cut off from a habitual drinking or drug habit. Typically, the person undergoes bouts of sweating and chills, with goose bumps (technically called *horripilation*) appearing on the skin. Anyone who has seen a plucked turkey prepared for the oven, its dead-white skin showing the pimplelike areas where the feathers have been removed, will at once understand the image.

COME UP TO SCRATCH

Formerly, in pugilistic contests, it was the practice to scratch a line across the ring which the fighters were to step over to begin the match or a round. Those who wavered did not *come up to (the) scratch* and were found wanting in courage and the other attributes necessary to a sound thrashing.

CORN-STEALER

A nineteenth-century slang word for the 'human hand.' Also called **lunch-hook.**

COWBOY

This word in the sense of 'a man on horseback who tends, rounds up, and drives cattle' is not attested till the late nineteenth century. In its earlier use, going back as far as 1779, it was applied to marauding bands of Tories that operated between the British and American lines during the Revolutionary War. Their object was the plundering of private property and the robbing of patriots and redcoats alike. The earlier term for what we today call a cowboy was *cowherd* or *cowherd boy,* and it seems possible that the shift to *cowboy,* once its eighteenth-century meaning became historical, was a shortening of *cowherd boy* influenced by the older word *cowboy*. There is no evidence for words like *cowgirl, cowman, cow outfit, cow-puncher,* etc., before the 1870s. Indeed, the word *cow* as used for 'cattle' (rather than in the usual, confined sense of 'female of the ox family') is first cited in 1869 and, from the evidence, is an Americanism.

CROOK THE ELBOW or LITTLE FINGER

An American expression, dating from the early 1800s, meaning to 'drink, especially to excess,' *crook* being used in the sense of 'bend.'

CROWD THE MOURNERS

1. An Ozark expression meaning to 'act hastily or prematurely.' The metaphor, if not at once transparent, refers

to burying someone before he is dead (to which the clever reply is, "Why wait till the last minute?").
2. An expression that arose in the mid nineteenth century with the meaning 'pressure, bring (undue) pressure to bear,' (or, as they would say in England, "pressurize") (1859).

A CURATE'S EGG
This idiomatic phrase, often used in the form of a simile, *like a curate's egg*, was originally British but has become so popular since the early 1970s that it is now known almost everywhere. If anything, it has been overused and ought to be given a rest. It comes from a cartoon in *Punch* that ran in 1895: a curate, breakfasting at the home of his bishop, is served a sulfurously bad egg; "I'm afraid you've got a bad egg, Mr. Jones," says the bishop; "Oh, no, my lord," replies the sycophant, "I assure you! Parts of it are excellent!" It can be seen how a reference to a *curate's egg* might be universally applied to anything, for there are few things that are totally good—though that does not imply that few are totally bad. This is a fine illustration of two characteristics of many idioms in the language: they can spring from virtually any source at all; and they can be totally opaque—that is, unless the background story or explanation is given for the expression, or one is somehow able to derive the sense from the context, there is no way that its meaning can be derived from the elements that make it up.

CURRY FAVOR
Devotees of Indian cuisine may favor curry, but probably need not *curry favor* to get their share. The original of this expression is found in a fourteenth-century French fable,

Roman de Fauvel, in which *Fauvel;* a "fawn-colored horse" appeared as a symbol of cunning and deceit. The expression *curry Fauvel* came to mean 'act in an obsequious, fawning manner; to toady up to someone.' The English version later became *curry Favel,* and a brown-nosing sycophant came to be known as a *curry-favel.* As the word *favel* fell out of favor, it was replaced by *favor,* which sounded much like it, and in this form has survived to the present.

CUT A RUSTY
An Ozark idiom meaning to 'do something foolish or awkward; behave improperly.' It is said to come from *rustic,* as in cut up *rustic,* or 'behave like a country bumpkin,' but the conclusive evidence is lacking.

CUT THE MUSTARD
Almost invariably used in the negative—*he/she can't cut the mustard, that doesn't cut the mustard,* etc.—this popular American expression means 'come up to expectations; achieve some desired function, purpose, or level of performance.' Speculation as to its origin ranges from the literal to the distorted: some observers guess that its source is culinary, suggesting that it takes an adroit chef to 'cut'— that is, 'add in small quantities'—mustard (yes, the spice) into his gastronomic endeavors. To anyone who knows anything about simple home cooking, let alone being a chef, this is patent nonsense, for mustard is far from being a difficult or sensitive spice to use, and is used mostly in making sauces and salad dressings, a secondary duty often relegated to a sous-chef. The *Dictionary of American Regional English* records *cut* with the meaning 'beat or whip (eggs) vigorously.' Another theory is based on the assumption that *mustard* is a mispronunciation of *muster,* in the sense of a 'military review,' and that *cut the muster* was tantamount to 'pass inspection.' There is no evidence whatsoever for this view; moreover, *muster* is (and has long been) a common term in the military, and there is no justification to assume that it might be mispronounced. To add to the confusion, a third theory is offered here:

mustard seeds are very, very tiny, and cutting them (literally) would be no mean feat, not to say laborious and requiring great care and concentration. As mustard seed is usually ground to a powder, there is no reason to introduce mustard-seed cutting as an occupation requiring skill and dexterity, especially if it is created merely to satisfy the need for an etymology. *Cut* in the sense of 'succeed; surpass' (as in, *He simply can't cut it*) seems to be older than *cut the mustard* and occurs in British English. It is entirely possible, considering the way language sometimes works, that the *mustard* was added later, for rhythm, for euphony, or merely out of playfulness. The idiom does not appear in the 1909 edition of the *Century Dictionary & Cyclopedia* and may be of recent origin. The first citation recorded in the *OED Supplement* is from 1907. As always, there is another possibility, though it seems a bit farfetched. It is said that John XXII, pope from 1316 to 1334, who had a reputation as a sybarite and resided at Avignon, was so fond of mustard as a seasoning that he appointed his nephew *Moutardier* 'mustard maker' to his court. To this day, *moutardier* is used colloquially in French (according to the *Dictionary of Modern Colloquial French,* Hérail and Lovatt, Routledge & Kegan Paul, 1984) to mean 'big shot,' and appears in the expression, *se croire le premier moutardier du pape* 'to have a high opinion of oneself,' literally, 'to believe oneself the "premier moutardier" of the pope.' It is not impossible that a variation of this idiom, translated into English several centuries ago, gave rise to the (negative) form of *cut the mustard*—that is, one who cannot be or is not a moutardier is the opposite—an ineffectual, insignificant fellow. The sense would thus be based on sarcasm, for, whatever elevated opinion John XXII might have had about his *moutardier,* he was, after all, merely someone who mixed the mustard. A French word for 'blend' is *couper* (English 'cut'). French *couper à quelque chose* 'be able, capable of doing something' and *il n'y coupe pas* 'He doesn't seem able to cope' both seem related. So this explanation, though admittedly elaborate, is not necessarily as fanciful as it might appear at first glance.

CUT UP OLD ONES
This expression, from thieves' argot in the United States, means to 'reminisce about old times, relive the wonderful scores of yesteryear.' It probably comes from a reference to newspaper clippings.

D

DEAD MAN'S HAND

This is a nickname for a poker hand that, according to most sources, is a pair of aces and a pair of eights, according to some, jacks and eights. It got its name from the somewhat apocryphal tale that it was the hand held by Wild Bill Hickok when he was shot in the back by Jack McCall on August 2, 1876, in Deadwood, South Dakota. In the folklore of the West, especially of Western poker, it is taken as an omen of bad luck.

DEVIL'S LANE

An 'extremely narrow way formed by two fences that are almost side by side, so built by owners of lands that abut directly, with no road or lane between' (1872). It was so called, according to *Century Magazine* (1888) because it was viewed as "a monument of bad neighborhood."

DEVIL'S RIDING-HORSE

The 'praying mantis' (1899).

DIE WITH (ONE'S) BOOTS ON

In the old days of the West, this usually meant 'die while in the act of gunning someone else down,' the fate of many gunfighters. Boot Hill, the name given to the potter's field in many a Western town, was so called because its inhabitants had died wearing their boots. Today, if the expression is used, it is in jocular reference to a person's dying in the performance of his duty, though not, necessarily, as a result of it. It is doubtful that a citation could be found for the use of the phrase in reference to a woman.

DOUBLE IN BRASS

The meaning of this expression, now entirely metaphorical, is to 'perform a function or do a job in addition to one's regular work.' Thus, of a teacher who drives a taxi in his spare time it might be said that "he doubles in brass as a taxi driver"—in other words, the auxiliary function is almost always mentioned following *as*. Like the sources of many metaphorical expressions, its origin lies in the literal meaning of the phrase: the problem in determining its etymology lies in identifying the source, context, and meaning of the literal phrase. *Double in brass,* which may on the surface seem so obscure, comes from the circus— the "three-ring," not the "Maximus" type. Performers and other circus personnel whose main function might have been to ride a bicycle across a high wire, tame lions, or pack themselves, along with the rest of the troupe, into a tiny car, were often called upon to play in the band during the grand processional. If they couldn't play an instrument—say, a trumpet or slide trombone—they were pressed

into service to march in the band, pretending to tootle away; hence, they *doubled in brass*.

DOUGHBOY

The nickname given to American soldiers in World War II was *GI* or *GI Joe*. *Doughboy* is a relic from World War I, but it had its origins in the War Between the States. There are several tales told more than twice of the etymology of the term, one being that infantrymen wore white belts that had to be cleaned with pipe clay, called "dough." An equally apocryphal though slightly more plausible theory has it that the globular brass buttons on the infantrymen's uniforms resembled the doughnuts of the day (bearing in mind that the hole was not introduced into the edible doughnut till later in the nineteenth century).

DRESSED TO THE NINES

If the following etymology is correct for this everyday expression, it has been in the language since the fourteenth century: it is said to derive from *to then eyen*, in Middle English. The only problem with this deft analysis is that there is no evidence to support it, for the phrase is not attested that early: the first citation in the *OED* is for 1787, and one might justifiably expect one before that if it is, indeed, that ancient. *To the eyes*, as in "mortgaged to the eyes," not listed before the 1880s, means 'wholly, thoroughly, right up to there.' *Dressed to the nines*, however, means 'elaborately decked out,' which is not the same thing. Till some new linking evidence is uncovered, the etymologists will be stymied and the theories concerning its origin will remain speculative—and imaginative.

DROP GAME

In a fairly common confidence trick a wallet containing a thick wad of money is dropped (by the "dropper") in the path of an approaching stranger (the "sucker") and is picked up by a confederate just in front of the dupe. The confederate opens it, feigns surprise at the contents, and tells the victim that, as he is in a hurry to leave town, he will leave the wallet with him on the condition that he advertise for the owner and give him (the confederate) twenty dollars (or more). On collecting the money, the confederate absconds, and the stranger, on examining the wallet (or handbag), discovers it stuffed with play money (1845). See also **be left holding the bag** or **baby**.

DRUGSTORE COWBOY

As recently as the 1960s, that relic of the past, the drugstore, was still in evidence in the United States, both in small towns and in big cities. It consisted of a shop that sold (mainly) patent medicines, with a special department where a pharmacist prepared prescription drugs. Along one wall was a soda fountain—that is, a marble counter with fixed stools on one side for customers and, on the other, equipment consisting of refrigerated bins for ice cream, containers for various flavorings, fruit sauces, nuts, syrups, and so forth, and taps for sodas, plain or flavored. In later incarnations soda fountains also offered sandwiches and, for those who perhaps had partaken too enthusiastically of the fare, Bromo-Seltzer or Alka-Seltzer in their distinctive blue dispensers. Gradually, the American drugstore became a minisupermarket for all sorts of merchandise—paper goods, cosmetics, soaps, and, later, every manner of household goods. In the old days, teenagers would congregate at the soda fountain (in a drugstore as well as in what was called in New York City a candy store, little more than a small shop containing a soda fountain and offering smokers' supplies and accessories, candy bars, chewing gum, etc., and, usually, newspapers and magazines). As might be expected, the neighborhood drugstore-cum-soda fountain became the focal meeting place of young people, frequented after school and, sometimes, in the evenings. The young men who went to them would typically gather together to watch the girls go by, remarking to one another about a particularly outstanding feature of the passing scene. The term *cowboy* was applied to them in affectionate derision, for they seldom engaged in any activity more energetic than an ogle. Those who might have been inclined to more aggressive behavior would, at an earlier time, have been referred to as *wolves;* but the relatively tame activity of merely "hanging around" earned for these would-be lotharios an epithet no stronger than *drugstore cowboy,* at first denotatively, later on with a note of derogation. Soda fountains, less profitable than gondolas filled with every imaginable kind of product, have been replaced, and those who once spent their time in them have taken to haunting fast-food restaurants and shopping malls.

DRUM UP
In former times, before the practice of advertising in printed media became so common, traveling hawkers of various wares would enter a village in their wagons and attract an audience by beating a drum. These salesmen, called *drummers* till relatively recently, would pitch a tent and became known as *pitchmen* who *pitched* their products to prospective customers, in an attempt to *drum up* trade. These old-fashioned expressions have remained in the language despite the advent of other means of selling; in many states today, even door-to-door selling, formerly a useful and convenient way for a housewife who could not easily go to a town to shop for a wide variety of goods, has been outlawed.

DRY WILTS
A midwestern-southern phrase describing a 'state of advanced decrepitude, as from age.' Randolph and Wilson quote: "That old feller's got the dry wilts, an' he looks plumb foolish a-runnin' after them gals."

DUTCH TREAT, GO DUTCH
In the past, the Dutch suffered much criticism from the British, chiefly as a result of the rivalry between their nations during the seventeenth century. Many expressions have survived in which *Dutch* appears as a term of opprobrium or derogation: *Dutchman* a nautical term for a 'poorly made patch concealed by paint or other disguise';

Dutch uncle 'someone who rebukes or criticizes another'; *in Dutch* 'in trouble'; *Dutch bargain* 'an agreement made when the parties are drunk'; *Dutch courage* 'courage that comes from a liquor bottle'; *Dutch reckoning* 'a bad day's work,' etc. In the same vein is a *Dutch treat* 'a situation in which everyone pays his own way.' Originally, it referred to an invitation by a host who, instead of paying for his guests, made everyone pay for himself; but today, the sting has been removed from the phrase, and people specifically invited to *go Dutch* 'partake of a *Dutch treat*' are not offended.

E

EAGER BEAVER

Beavers are known not only for their remarkable engineering skills but for their industry, as well. This metaphor, applied to people more often than to beavers, probably became popular because it is a near-rhyme—certainly the vowel sounds of *eager* are more compatible with those of *beaver* than are those of *industrious*—and thus clichés are born.

EAR TO THE GROUND

Before the days when the sounds of traffic can be heard almost anywhere, when one jet after another scream overhead, when the nearby fire siren or burglar alarm cleave the air at all hours of the day and night, life was much quieter, and one might detect the approach of a horseman by literally putting his ear to the ground. This literal practice became a figurative expression, *keep one's ear to the ground* 'be alert to what might happen next, especially as foretold by rumor or some other sign' or *have one's ear to the ground* 'be in a continuous state of alertness for any relevant news.'

EAT HUMBLE PIE

Although this idiom, having the sense of 'demean or humiliate oneself' (as in making an abject apology) looks as though *humble* implies "humility," its origin is quite different. The older English word for the entrails of a deer—heart, liver, kidneys, etc., classed together as offal—was *numbles*. This was often baked into a meat pie called *numble pie*. When one referred to *a numble pie* it was difficult to tell if he was saying that or *an umble pie,* which, among *h*-dropping Londoners, would have been the way of saying what an upper-class speaker would call *a humble pie*. This problem worked both ways in English: sometimes a word beginning with a vowel preceded by *an* would adopt the *n* as its own. That happened with a *newt,* which was originally *an eft,* then suffered a migrating *n* to become *a newt*. Curiously, *eft* and *newt* exist side by side in English (especially the English of crossword puzzles). Another, similar pair: *napery* 'linens in general' yielded *a napron* 'a particular application of linen for keeping the clothing from getting soiled.' The *n* migrated, resulting in *an apron*. (But note that the *n* remained on its native ground not only in *napery* but in *napkin,* in which the *-kin* is a diminutive suffix.) Another example of *n*-migration is seen in the word *nickname*. Those who remember the Prologue from Chaucer's Canterbury Tales may recall the lines:

Whan Zephirus eke with his swete breth
Inspired hath in ev'ry holt and heeth
The tendre croppes . . .

Eke, a common Middle English word, meant 'also' in many contexts, though in the extract above it might be better rendered as 'quite'; it is not related to the *eke* used in *eke out a meager existence*. In the fourteenth century people talked about *eke-names* 'also-names': a man's name might be John, but because he was a carpenter, his *eke-name* was "Carpenter." While the sense of *eke-name* gradually changed, so did its form. Originally, people spoke about an *eke-name;* later, bearing in mind that there was little writing— the printing press did not have much effect on western European culture till about 1500—and that literacy was low, there was not much support from the spelled form for an *eke-name,* and the *n* gradually migrated over, creating *a neke-name,* today spelled *nickname*. Other examples of the migrating *n* are *an adder* from *a nadder* and *an auger* from *a nauger*.

EIGHTY-SIX

There is a conventional number-language used in short-order restaurants across the United States. It probably evolved because the pronunciation of a number shouted above the din of diners, clattering dinnerware, clinking glasses, tinkling "silverware"—to say nothing of the cacophony of orders yelled over the noise of broken crockery and glassware—can be heard and understood more easily than, "May I please have a cup of coffee with cream?" (commonly rendered as *Draw one, white*). Someone wisely introduced some order into the noonday chaos of luncheonettes by inventing a code, some elements of which have become conventional:

   86: 'We don't have any more.'
   81: 'One glass of water.'
   82: 'Two glasses of water.' (. . . etc., up to eighty-five)

Eighty-six has spilled over into the general language to mean 'There isn't/aren't any more,' partly because many people at one time or another in their youth worked part-time in a fast-food restaurant, diner, or other, similar place after school; others, who never had such jobs, could not help learning the system because they were exposed to it frequently as customers. As far as is known, there has not been a national study of the language of the luncheonette, so the universality of such extralinguistic codes is not well documented. There are a few lexical items that are well known, some of them clearly created to avoid confusion, others out of mere playfulness:

   Adam and Eve on a raft: 'Ham and eggs'
   Adam and Eve on a raft—wreck 'em: 'Ham and scrambled eggs'
   Burn one: 'One hamburger' (or 'One chocolate milkshake')

EIGHTY

B.L.T. (down): 'Bacon, lettuce, and tomato sandwich (on toast)'
Black and white: 'Chocolate soda with vanilla ice cream'

There are probably many more, especially regional expressions; and it is interesting to note that this private language seems to be exclusively an American phenomenon.

F

FIG, NOT WORTH A

There are several English idioms dealing with figs: *not worth a fig; a fig for him; give a fig; the fig of Spain,* and others. Curiously, figs figure in similar expressions in Latin, French, Spanish, German, Italian, and other Indo-European languages. In Classical Greek they seem to have been used in a different application, *to know figs from cardamom* was the same as *to know chalk from cheese.* Little is known about the origin of *fig* in Indo-European: it has been traced to Latin *ficus* and (cognate) Greek *sykon,* but there the trail ends, though one investigator speculates a Hebrew, another a "Mediterranean" origin. What captures one's interest in this word is less the origin of its form than the ineluctable fact that figs have for millennia been regarded as very sexy objects. This may seem somewhat perverse to those whose familiarity with the fruit is limited to its appearance, in dried form, squeezed among others into a box or ring-shaped pack with "Smyrna" and other exotic names printed on its foil label. But in Greek *sykon* was used—though not exclusively, of course—to refer to the *pudenda muliebria.* In Latin and down through Romance as well as Germanic, *fig* referred to a gesture of a fist with the thumb protruding from between two of the clenched fingers; it also designates the gesture of putting the thumb in the mouth; and, sometimes, it is used for the derisive gesture of flicking the thumbnail against the upper front teeth, palm outward. These gestures, called *give a fig* (or, in French, *faire la figue* and in Spanish *dar la higa*) are insulting and obscene; they can be rendered in English as symbols for *fuck you, up yours,* etc., expressions and sentiments scarcely likely to win friends and influence people (except adversely). It seems probable that the sense 'something insignificant' in *not worth a fig* and *not care a fig* comes from the same semantic shift that occurs with English *fuck: I don't give a fuck* (or, in extended form, *I don't give a flying fuck at a rolling doughnut*), *fuck-all* 'nothing,' and other expressions employing words like *fuck* (as well as *shit*) in the sense of 'something of no value or consideration.' It seems, too, that the wood of the fig tree is spongy and of no useful application; the Classical Greek phrase *sykenoi andres* means 'worthless men.' When one encounters fresh figs growing or even in a market, it becomes clear why their visual appearance has given rise to so many translinguistic metaphors: not to mince words, a pair of fresh figs closely resembles, in size and configuration, a pair of testicles. Pressed together, they resemble the external parts of the female genitalia. The gesture described above, of the thumb protruding from between the clenched fingers of the fist, means, simply, 'fuck you.' In addition to their appearance, certain figs, especially those of the common and popular Smyrna variety, can be fertilized only by a method called *caprification,* in which fruits are hung in trees to attract a particular insect, the fig wasp, which is the only means by which such figs are (naturally) pollinated. *Caprification* comes from Latin *capri-* (the combining form of *caper* 'goat') and the *fic-* of *ficus*—that is, not the *fic-* from Latin *facere* 'do, make,' which appears in thousands of words like *mortification, codification, magnification,* etc. This (Smyrna) fig is called the *caprifig,* from Latin *caprificus* 'wild fig tree,' but it is unclear whether the *capri-* is used in the sense of 'wild' or in some sexual sense, for goats have always been associated closely with lasciviousness. In light of the preceding, one might be tempted to make some connection between *fig* and *fuck,* for which the etymology is not complete, but there is too little justification for that without further evidence.

FISHING EXPEDITION

This modern American metaphor, referring to 'any sort of informal exploratory investigation, particularly one in which the investigator has no preconceived notion of what will be found,' may have its origins in the older expression, *fishing voyage,* which dates back to 1682 *(DAE)* and referred, literally, to any extended sea voyage, especially one to the Grand Banks, off Newfoundland. In general use, it today implies an activity attributed to a detective, tax inspector, or other official who digs around seeking (possibly incriminating) evidence but without more to go on than his suspicions that some wrongdoing has taken place. Occasionally, but not usually, it is used to refer merely to a random search, as for investors in an enterprise: *He went on a fishing expedition to raise capital for the new venture.*

FISH STORY

A 'cock-and-bull story': the term refers to the characteristic tall tales told by fishermen about "the one that got away" (1819). Such claims are said to be *fishy* (1840).

FIVE-O'CLOCK SHADOW

The 'darkish shade that appears toward the end of the day on the chin and cheeks of a man who shaved before going to work in the morning.' It was coined by the copywriters who prepared the advertising campaign for Gem blades during the late 1930s/early 1940s and suggested that a closer shave could be obtained by using their product, thus avoiding *five o'clock shadow.*

FOR KEEPS

Originally a children's term meaning 'seriously,' this idiom refers to the rules under which a game may be played: in marbles, for example, when one plays *for fun,* the marbles won are returned to the players who lost them; when one plays *for keeps,* the winner(s) keep(s) all those won.

FOR THE BIRDS

The sparrows and pigeons that are seen in most cities survive on next to nothing, the meager crumbs they can glean from the pavements seem to be so scanty, notwithstanding the occasional feast provided now and then by a bird fancier. This state of affairs has reinforced the sense of paucity suggested by the expression *for the birds*. The original sense was probably rooted in two other characteristics of bird nourishment: first, the fact that the chickens kept in the farmyard were usually fed scraps from the table and other items, like stale bread, for which people had no further use; the insignificance of this fare is expressed also in the term *chickenfeed*. Secondly, everyone has seen how sparrows and other seed-eating birds pick through horse droppings to find and eat the undigested oats. The replacement of horses by the horseless carriage has markedly reduced the availability of this source of nourishment, but the notion of a creature's using horse manure as its food source has remained. Thus, *for the birds* is today used to mean 'totally unacceptable, below contempt' on the one hand and 'insignificant, paltry' on the other.

G

GARRISON FINISH

This American idiom means 'any close finish.' It is now applied metaphorically to any kind of contest—competitors for a job might be said to be in a *Garrison finish*—but the expression originated at the racetrack and is named after a jockey who favored the practice of holding back his mount till the last minute, when he would drive it onward to win, using the horse's reserve energy for the final thrust.

GERRYMANDER

This word is what linguists call a *blend,* though some follow Lewis Carroll in calling it a *portmanteau,* which is another name for the same thing. Elbridge Gerry was the governor of Massachusetts from 1810 to 1812. For the (annual) gubernatorial election of 1812 he succeeded in maneuvering the reorganization of voting districts in such a way as to concentrate votes so that he might win. Curiously, a map of the redrawn voting districts formed a jagged, sinuous path in Essex County. The story goes that Gilbert Stuart, the well-known painter, visited the offices of the *Centinel* newspaper, which was opposed to Gerry, and, seeing the map on the wall in the editor's office, drew in a head, wings, claws, and tail of a dragon. The result, said Stuart, was a salamander; "Gerrymander is more like it," retorted the editor, and so a new word sprang into being. Gerry was defeated. In his defense it must be said that although he has received a bad press for the redistricting maneuver, it was not only common practice at the time but common enough since to have allowed the word *gerrymander* to survive. Gerry, born in 1744, was an American patriot, signer of the Declaration of Independence, Congressman, and governor of Massachusetts, among other accomplishments. In 1812, he was elected Vice President of the United States under James Madison, and died in office in 1814.

GET THE SHORT END OF THE STICK

This common Americanism, which means to 'be left with the greater (or greatest) burden, get the worst of a deal,' is said by the *Dictionary of American Slang* to come from getting the end of a stick poked up one's rectum by one in command of a situation, who holds the other end. This seems an unusually stern method for controlling another person; it seems improbable that the expression arose from an actual practice—but people are peculiar, and one never can be sure. Without giving the origin of the expression much (penetrating) thought, one might assume that it had something to do with drawing the short straw—that is, ending up as the unlucky one merely by chance. In *American Speech* (Winter, 1986), Professor James B. McMillan of the University of Alabama offers another theory, dredged up from a 1973 number of a newsletter published by a local (Alabaman) historical society:

> Men lined up on both sides of the log. They stuck strong sticks under the log and a man took hold of each end of the stick to raise the log and carry it off the field. Both men were to walk close to the log. If one man held the stick some distance from the log, that threw excessive weight on the other man who held the stick close to the log. From this came the expression "getting the short end of the stick."

On the "neatness" scale, this etymology is more plausible than the somewhat less savory rectal explanation. Yet there are a few nagging inconsistencies: first of all, there would have to have been (at least) two sticks under the log—not fewer than four men—to lift and carry the log; second, if getting the short end of the stick was a frequent enough occurrence to allow the expression to become a cliché, why hadn't the log carriers long since used shorter sticks, thereby preventing one man from holding his end at a distance from the log? Like many other expressions in the language, this does not yield quite so readily to what may, on the surface, appear to be a pat analysis.

GHOST WALKS, THE
This is theater slang for 'salaries are paid.' It is said to have originated with a troupe that was rehearsing *Hamlet*, in which Hamlet says, in reference to his father's ghost, "Perchance 'twill walk again" (I, ii, 242). A member of the cast, who were unpaid, answered, "No, I'm damned if the ghost walks till salaries are paid."

GIVE SOMEONE or GET THE BIRD
It may seem odd that a bad act *gets the bird* by having the audience issue catcalls, but it all becomes clear when one learns that the original expression was *get* (or *give*) *the big bird,* and that the *big bird* was a goose. Geese hiss when they are angry or disturbed, which is just what an unappreciative audience does.

GO BY THE BOARD
Another one of many expressions having a nautical origin, this one, which means to 'be gone, or lost,' refers to the *board* of *overboard:* mast and rigging gone by the board have been washed into the sea, not to be recovered.

GO HAYWIRE
Charles Earle Funk, no mean etymologist and, unlike some modern scholars, a man with his ear to the ground, confuted the origin of this Americanism as given in H. L. Mencken's *The American Language, Supplement One.* Mencken suggested that the expression acquired its sense of 'chaotic disorder' from the wild whipping about of baling wire (that is, *haywire*) when a bale of hay is opened by cutting the wire with the blow of a hatchet. Funk argues

that notwithstanding the leaping ends of the cut wire when released from tension, the term comes from the application of used haywire to the repair of farm tools and other equipment, implying that because baling wire rusts easily and is generally an inferior product it is somewhat infra dig for any farmer to make extensive use of it. Thus, according to his book, *A Hog on Ice & Other Curious Expressions,* Funk holds that a place in which such rusty patches of wire are in common sight has *gone haywire.* That does nothing to explain either the expression *go haywire* (as a present active verb) nor the current meaning, to 'behave in an uncontrolled manner.' This may be a later, derived sense, and Funk may be right; but he also writes that the idiom is of twentieth-century origin, making it about thirty years old when Mencken wrote about it and about fifty when Funk's book came out. *Go haywire* does seem to mean 'act uncontrolledly,' and Mencken's analysis would appear to be the more plausible one.

GOOD-ENOUGH MORGAN

A political expression from the early eighteenth century referring to any maneuver or ploy that can be turned to advantage temporarily to influence voters. William Morgan disappeared on September 12, 1826, on the eve of the publication of his book that was said to reveal all of the secrets of Masonry. It was commonly assumed that he had been kidnapped and spirited away by Masons, and Antimasonic sentiment was strengthened. Thurlow Weed (1797–1882), a prominent Antimason, coined the phrase (1827), which was used metaphorically: "It is reported that people, who had obtained all the political objects desired from the impression that the body was Morgan's, observed 'that he was a good enough Morgan, until after the election.' " (*Western Missouri Review,* 1829)

GO OFF HALF-COCKED

This old expression goes back to the use of the flintlock of the eighteenth century. This gun was loaded by pouring powder down the muzzle, then packing in the projectile, usually a lead ball. It was equipped with a flint and steel, on a spring contrivance at the breech. When the hammer was retracted (that is, cocked) and then released by the trigger, the flint was struck against the steel, creating a spark that ignited the powder, propelling the bullet through the barrel to the target. Sometimes, the flint would snap forward onto the steel and ignite the powder before the hammer was fully retracted, and the gun would *go off half-cocked* or *at half cock*. One did not aim a gun while it was being cocked, so if it went off prematurely, the bullet went wide of its mark, missing the target completely. This gave rise to the metaphor *go off half-cocked* which means to 'take sudden, irrational action that has no aim or direction.'

In an earlier type of gun, before the flintlock became the weapon of "modern" warfare, the powder was ignited at the breech by placing a small amount of powder into a small pan fitted alongside the breech. This, ignited by a hand-held flint and steel, acted as a primer for igniting the main charge, which exploded and drove the bullet out of the barrel. Sometimes, the powder in the pan would ignite but fail to light the powder in the gun. This was called a *flash in the pan,* which has come down into Modern English in the sense of 'anything that makes a show of functioning as it should but is completely ineffectual; temporary, spectacular effort that yields no result or an insignificant one at best.'

GRASS ROOTS

This common idiom, often used in political contexts, refers to the people who are regarded as the basic mainstay of the population—that is, it excludes the more sophisticated, professional, and urban(e) population. Earlier, its meaning was confined to rural population, its original application stemming from a literal reference to grass roots, and, indeed, anyone who has had first-hand experience with lawns will readily see the connection between the tenacity of grass roots for the soil and that of those segments of the population involved in farming. In some contexts it has lately been extended in use to include those members of a political party or faction who are not in a position of power, similar to *rank and file*.

GRASS WIDOW
Modern life has produced widows of every category, from **California widows** *(q.v.),* whose husbands disappeared out West to seek their fortunes in the gold fields in the 1850s, to *golf widows,* whose husbands vanish with some regularity to drive a small white ball before them across a more-or-less well-manicured lawn in their attempts at making it drop into a hole, whence they retrieve it to strike it again with their oddly shaped clubs. A late twentieth-century reflex of the same phenomenon is the *computer widow,* whose husband works late at the office, exterminating the bugs and other vermin that disrupt the smooth operation of those devices. A *grass widow,* however, is not a woman whose husband has succumbed to overzealous concern for his lawn nor one whose spouse has become addicted to marijuana: she is merely, in modern American usage, a 'divorcée,' formerly 'a woman separated from her husband temporarily.' The term sprang from an old euphemism for an unmarried woman who has a child, *grass* referring to the site where the child was born (or conceived). Parallel expressions appear in many North Germanic languages.

GREEK TO ME, IT'S
Used in the sense 'meaningless,' this old expression might have antedated Shakespeare. But there is a good citation for it in *Julius Caesar* (I,ii):

CASSIUS: Did Cicero say anything?
CASCA: Ay, he spoke Greek.
CASSIUS: To what effect?
CASCA: Nay, an I tell you that, I'll ne'er look you in the face again; but those that understood him smiled at one another and shook their heads; but, for mine own part, it was Greek to me.

See also **gringo.**

GREEN-GOODS MAN

An obsolete American slang term for a 'counterfeiter' (1888).

GRINGO

This is an uncomplimentary—contemptuous might be more descriptive—name given by Spanish-speaking peoples to a foreigner who speaks no Spanish. It is commonly thought that it originated in Mexico in the 1840s, during the Mexican War, but there is evidence for its use in Spain in the eighteenth century, and it is recorded in a Spanish dictionary of 1787, indicating its established use at the time. Theories as to the origin of *gringo* include (as quite likely) its being a corrupted form of *griego* 'Greek,' which would provide an interesting link with the expression (**it's**) **Greek to me** *(q.v.)*.

GRIN LIKE A CHESHIRE CAT

It may come as a disappointment to many, but Lewis Carroll was not the originator of the Cheshire cat: indeed, to his contemporaries, the embodiment of the Cheshire cat (and its fleeting bouts with disembodiment) was (and was supposed to be) humorous—a manifest pun. The phrase well established at the time was *grin like a Cheshire cat*. The *OED* offers no guidance to the etymology; E. Cobham Brewer, in *The Dictionary of Phrase & Fable,* suggests that there was a cheese made in Cheshire molded in a form that resembled a grinning cat. Taking a clue from this theory, one might speculate further: *cat* was, in addition to its designation of 'feline,' a term for a wide variety of things of different shapes; more appropriately, *cate* was an old word meaning 'delicacy,' usually found in the plural, *cates*. Turning to *grin,* that word could mean 'snare, trap' or 'harness.' It is possible—anything is possible in etymology—that the Cheshire cheeses were done up in string bags (like some cheeses today), or *grins,* and that the original phrase was something like *grin of (a) Cheshire cate,* meaning a 'string bag of the Cheshire delicacy.' It would be an easy step from *grin of* to *grin like* given the playfulness of speakers of English.

H

HAIR OF THE DOG
Usually heard in this form, this expression is a shortening of *hair of the dog that bit you,* a metaphoric reference to homeopathic medical practice in which a cure for an affliction is based on (or closely associated with) its cause or origin. Thus, someone unfortunate enough to have been bitten by a rabid dog could presumably be cured of rabies by an antidote prepared from that same dog's hair. There is evidence to show that the expression has long been used metaphorically rather than literally, and its meaning today has been narrowed down to refer specifically to a 'hangover cure achieved by taking a nip of the same potion that brought on the hangover.'

HANGING BEE
This facetious term for a 'lynching' goes back to 1836. See also **bee.**

HANG THE LANDLADY
An obsolete (1902) expression meaning to 'abscond without paying,' applied to "moonshining" activities. Its origin is not certain, but it may have come from "let the landlady go hang for the money owed."

HANG THE MOON
An Ozark Mountain phrase used to signify an individual of great importance. It is equivalent to "he's God or the power that created and arranged the heavens." It occurs

in expressions like *In her eyes he's so wonderful she thinks he hung the moon.*

HAPPY AS A CLAM (AT HIGH TIDE or WATER)

'Supremely happy.' Perhaps the curving edge of a hard clam *(Venus mercenaria)* resembles a smile; it is difficult to discern bivalve emotions and to imagine why clams, which by nature are buried in the littoral earth both below and above low-water marks, should necessarily be less than joyful at low tide, till one takes into account the fact that at high tide the clam may be safer from the predations (of man) than at low tide.

HARD AND FAST

This phrase is firmly fixed in the language, often attached to *rule:* a *hard and fast rule* in the sense 'unalterable.' Its origin is nautical; it refers to a vessel that is stuck on the bottom, which is hard, where it is held fast—that is, not the *fast* that means 'quick.' See also **touch and go.**

HARLOT

The etymology of this word is quite straightforward—it was borrowed into Middle English from Old French *herlot* 'fellow, rogue'—but it did undergo a curious sexual and moral transformation in the course of its meanderings through about six centuries of use. One of its earlier senses became specialized to refer to a 'traveling performer, juggler, entertainer,' and it became first androgynous, then transsexual. By the sixteenth century, it had come to be used as a less offensive variant of *whore,* though in the same sense. The anecdote is told about the time, in the 1930s, when Lady Margot Asquith, British author and widow of Prime Minister Herbert Henry Asquith, found herself in the company of Jean Harlow. The platinum-blonde movie star was forward enough to address her by her given name, mispronouncing it to rhyme with *marplot.* "The t," offered Lady Asquith, "is silent, as in Harlow."

HAVE A BONE IN HER TEETH

The "her" refers to a 'vessel, especially a sailing vessel, which is moving along at a great clip in a favorable, usually a quartering, breeze.' The "bone" refers to the white foam that appears at the bows of such a vessel as she courses happily over the main. It is an expression today used by yachtsmen.

HELLBENT FOR . . .

Hellbent for . . . appears with any number of "destinations" that can be filled into the slot: *hellbent for election, hellbent for trouble, hellbent for disaster*—in short, it is what might be called a "do-it-yourself" idiom. In all, *hellbent* is the transposed phrase *bent for hell* in which *bent* means 'determined; destined.' In other words, one who is *hellbent on* or *for* something is behaving as if he is determined to do it or get there despite the fires of hell. The expression *hellbent for leather* 'going at breakneck speed' is a Westernism, the leather referring to horseriding gear, but is not restricted to speed on horseback: any rapid means of movement will do. It is sometimes shortened to *hell for leather*.

HIS NAME IS MUD

Whose name? Mudd's, of course. It was a Dr. Samuel Mudd who treated John Wilkes Booth's leg, broken when he leapt onto the stage of the Ford's Theater, in Washington, on the night of April 14, 1865, after assassinating President Abraham Lincoln. Booth escaped in the confusion and made his way to Dr. Mudd's office, nearby, and was patched up. Mudd did not know that Booth had shot the president till the following day, when the news came out, whereupon he immediately called the authorities.

Notwithstanding, he was arrested, tried as a conspirator, and convicted, sentenced to spend the rest of his life in prison. Years later he was pardoned by President Andrew Johnson for helping to stop an outbreak of yellow fever at the prison. His name, shortened in spelling, had already become a cliché of the day for 'anyone infamous,' though today Mudd is forgotten as the eponymic source of the expression, and it remains for books like this one to stir up dead prejudices.

HOBSON'S CHOICE
Tobias Hobson, the operator of a livery stable in Cambridge, England, followed an irrevocable policy of offering customers who hired a horse the one nearest the stable door—take it or leave it. Thus, *Hobson's choice* came to mean 'no choice at all: either take the first thing offered or take nothing.' Hobson flourished (if that is the proper term) in the seventeenth century and was commemorated by Milton in epitaphs.

HOG LATIN
See **pig Latin**.

A HOG ON ICE
To many Americans, this expression is known only from the title of a book by Charles Earle Funk, *A Hog on Ice & Other Curious Expressions*, published in 1948 (reissued by Harper & Row in 1985). It smacks of the farm, but, according to Funk, who zealously tracked down its origins to Revolutionary times in America and to the seventeenth century in England, Ireland, and Scotland, it was in common use throughout the eastern states around the end of the nineteenth century, off the farm as well as on. Even when one learns that the fuller expression is a simile, *as independent as a hog on ice*, the sense is obscure: those ignorant of hog behavior wonder why the animal should be so characterized. An official of the U.S. Department of Agriculture went so far as to explain why a hog on ice should evoke an image of independence. A citation that

provides yet more context—*as independent as a hog on ice; if I can't stand up I can lay down*—is equally unilluminating. On investigation, Funk turned up the information that Englishmen do not use the word *hog* for farm animals; they use *pig*. So he searched further and discovered that *hog* is the name given in the game of curling to a stone when it comes to rest. His delight at this find was short-lived, for not only is this curling hog removed from play at once, but it is not readily apparent why independence should be associated with it: after all, independence is a human characteristic, sometimes attributed to animals (like Kipling's cat), but only rarely to inanimate objects. Later, though, having exhausted all other avenues of investigation, Funk returned to his "curling" theory:

> If this hypothesis be correct, then the very fact that the stone occupied a central position, showing no regard to its interference with subsequent players, like an automobile driver who "hogs" the center of a road, made it appear self-assured, cocky, and independent, and thus gave rise to the humorous simile that came down through the centuries.

This suggests that the removal of the hog in curling was a later development in the rules of the game, and that originally, at least when the expression was coined, it was still very much an obstacle to the players.

HOIST WITH or BY ONE'S OWN PETARD

Petard was the word for an explosive charge, something like a grenade, used to blow off a door or to open a hole in a wall. *To be hoisted by one's own petard* once meant to be 'blown up by one's own explosive device'; today it is used metaphorically to 'suffer the consequences of the fate one has designed for others.' The word *petard* itself offers some opportunity for amusing fantasy, for it comes from French *péter* 'to break wind' and, in plain English, a *petard* is a *fart*. Thus, if taken in its original, literal sense, the image is quite funny. (Which is why so much of language cannot be taken in its original, literal sense: language is a very, very serious business, as can be seen from this example.)

(NOT) HOLD A CANDLE TO

This common expression, which means 'be comparable with or to,' has a traditionally recognized origin: in sixteenth-century England, those who went abroad in the city at night were accompanied by a servant who carried a candle to light the way (as there was no street lighting); the servant who performed this duty was at a pretty low level in the domestic hierarchy, so one who was even lower than the low was considered unfit to hold a candle to (or for) his master. On the face of it, this seems an unacceptably thin explanation for, as far as is known, such servants carried torches, or links, and were called *link-boys*: after all, what could one see by the feeble light of a candle? Moreover, such a lighting device would have to have been in a lantern, so we might expect an expression like "hold a lantern to"; and, finally, why *to* instead of *for*? It is known that people "talked funny" in the sixteenth century, but not that funny. It seems more likely that the idiom arose from a confusion of two earlier expressions. One, attested from the fifteenth century, refers to votive candles and appears in the old expression *hold a candle to the devil* 'propitiate the devil'; the other, with which it was confused, refers to the minor servant charged with the responsibility of holding a candle for his master while he worked at something, thus, 'be in a menial position to' someone. This latter sense is taken as the literal origin of the idiom in the *OED*. In modern applications, it occurs only in the negative: *When it comes to repairing watches, no one can hold a candle to George.*

HOODLUM

One of the delights of word archaeology is that its pursuit often reveals the lengths to which the human imagination—or credulity—can be stretched. Although there are many words and phrases the origins of which are sufficiently well documented to occasion nothing more than routine acceptance, there are many about which little is known and which offer to the creative mind the opportunity to create a veritable phantasmagoria of theories as to their sources. The word *hoodlum* has been subjected to virtually every linguistic test devisable by man, from the idea that it is a distortion (of course) of a dialectal Bavarian word, *hodalump,* to that of a Pidgin English phrase, *hoodlahnt* 'very lazy mandarin,' to the attribution of a Spanish source (unidentified). There is even a theory that the word is from the family name spelled *Muldoon* backward, with the *n* to *h* shift explained as a scribal error. About the only fact agreed on by all is that the word surfaced around 1870 in San Francisco. There the subject must rest till further evidence can be found: perhaps it is an anagram, coined by a mad scientist, from *loud* 'noisy' + *mho* 'unit of conductance' because *hoodlums* were originally loudmouthed San Francisco tourist guides. See also **hooligan.**

BY HOOK OR BY CROOK

A *hook* is just what it sounds like; a *crook* is a staff with a hooklike end. This expression, which means 'by one means or another,' is the result of a combination of words that mean almost the same thing and have been brought together because they rhyme. There are other compounds and phrases, common in the language, that have survived because they are alliterative, rhyming, or rhythmically pleasing: *spic and span; hunky dory; rack and ruin; sink or swim; healthy, wealthy, and wise; slender, tender, and tall; willy-nilly; niminy-piminy; namby-pamby; pell-mell; highways and byways,* etc.

HOOLIGAN

Unlike **hoodlum** *(q.v.)* (which, in the fanciful world of etymology, is seriously proposed as *hooligan* pronounced by someone with a speech defect), *hooligan* seems to be well enough documented as derived from the Irish name *Houlihan,* "which came to be associated with rowdies," according to *The Random House Unabridged Dictionary*. The

OED, which traces the word back to 1898, suggests that it might have come from *Hooley's gang* (presumably a band of ruffians—Irish, of course), with frequent support from a music-hall song of the time, "Hooligan." While these theories illustrate the depths to which etymologists will descend in order to arrive at a believable origin for a word, they grasp at straws and do not provide the sort of incontrovertible evidence sought by ardent word historians. To be sure, one of the more colorful uses of the word occurred in the film, *The Asphalt Jungle,* in reference to a ruffian of the lowest order of criminals (played by Sterling Hayden) who was recruited to serve as the patsy for a crime to be committed by a gang headed by a "genius" who, obviously, comes to a bad end.

HOOTCHY-KOOTCHY
This fanciful name for a suggestive oriental dance is first attested (in the *OED*) in 1895, in one of Finley Peter Dunne's "Mr. Dooley" columns, which makes it an Americanism. Dunne did not coin the word—though he was certainly capable of doing so—because it appears in a song about the Chicago Columbian Exposition of 1892 (which commemorated the four hundredth anniversary of Columbus's landing in the New World). One of the themes of the exposition was associated with Egypt, which was not inappropriate, as the area south of Chicago seems to have been influenced in its place-naming, for instance, of Cairo (which is pronounced CARE-oh in Illinois). In 1893, James Thornton (1861-1938), songwriter and occasional vaudeville performer, wrote a song, "The Streets of Cairo," inspired after seeing Little Egypt, a hootchy-kootchy dancer at the fair. It became popular at once and, although few know the lyrics, the music is well known as that to which the risqué lyrics "Oh, they don't wear pants/ In the southern part of France . . ." are sung. (Thornton's early education, in Boston, was guided by Henry Wadsworth Longfellow; he later became a friend and drinking companion of John L. Sullivan's and toured the vaudeville circuit with Charles B. Lawlor, who wrote "The Sidewalks

of New York." Thornton's other hits included "My Sweetheart's the Man in the Moon" (1892) and "When You Were Sweet Sixteen" (1898). None of this has even the remotest connection with *hootchy-kootchy,* of course, but it seems worth telling, nonetheless.) Some of Thornton's lyrics (quoted from memory) are:

> I will sing you a song,
> And it won't take very long,
> 'Bout a maiden fair
> With a wealth of golden hair.

> She lived out the city
> Oh, and what a pity,
> Poor little maiden.
> She had never seen the streets of Cairo;
> On the Midway* she had never been;
> She had never seen the hootchy-kootchy.
> —Poor little country maid!

The source of *hootchy-kootchy,* which appears in a number of variant spellings, has not been determined. It is clearly what linguists would call a rhyming reduplicative formation. There is no evidence for a word *hootchy* or *hootch,* and *hooch,* a slang word for 'whisky' taken from an American Indian language, seems too remote semantically to prove a likely candidate. One variant is *cooch,* and the form *cooch dancer,* a 'woman who performs the hootchy-kootchy,' also occurs. The sources searched yield only *nautch* ('dancer'), which is close, but no adequate explanation for the switch from the *n*-sound to the *k*-sound is available. If there is a valid etymological source, it has not yet turned up; till it does, the origin of *hootchy-kootchy* will have to be considered another enigma associated with the Mysterious East.

HORN-MAD

'Very furious, indeed; enraged'—like a bull, in other words. That is certainly one possibility. Another is the condition

---

*Midway was the name of the main thoroughfare at the exposition.

of a husband who has been cuckolded, in which *horn* takes on quite a different meaning. Although the *Century Dictionary* gives only the former sense, the citations given would seem to favor the latter:

horn-mad:
"Keep him from women, he thinks h' has
lost his mistress;
And talk of no silk stuffs, 'twill run him horn-mad."
(Fletcher, *The Pilgrim,* iii,7)

horn-madness:
"Somebody courts your wife, Count?
Where and when?
How and why? Mere horn–madness: have a care."
(Browning, *The Ring and the Book,* II,832.)

Though accepting that the literal (cattle) sense is somewhat out of date, the *OED* labels the cuckold sense obsolete. It is useful to note that this section of these dictionaries was prepared at approximately the same time—the mid-1880s—but it must be borne in mind that the *OED,* reflecting American usage to some extent, was researched and written by British editors, while the *Century* was essentially American.

HORSE LATITUDES

Referring to the 'area of the Atlantic Ocean between the prevailing easterlies (trade winds) to the south and the westerlies to the north,' this name for the doldrums has at least two suggested origins. One holds that during the eighteenth century, when ships from the Old World were becalmed in these waters, the horses (and cattle) they were carrying died and had to be jettisoned. The credibility of that explanation would rely on the habitual loss of cargo for such an expression to arise, and the image of a persistently large number of horse carcasses floating about in the sea is a bit hard to accept. The other theory set forth is that the region is so named after the Spanish *El Golfo de las Yeguas* 'Gulf of the Mares,' so called from its "unruly and boisterous nature." One cannot have it both ways—

calm and boisterous—so another explanation might have to be sought. Indeed, the reference to *El Golfo de las Yeguas* has been searched for and not found: it does not appear in any modern gazetteer, and older works, from the nineteenth century, yield no results. The extensive map library at the British Library has yielded no reference, nor have the files of the Permanent Committee on Geographic Names (Royal Geographical Society). The citation quoted in the *OED* is from a work on meteorology dated 1883, but the author quotes a "Mr. Laughton" in giving the attribution, and the gulf in question seems to have existed entirely in Mr. Laughton's mind.

HUNKY DORY

The source books are uniformly silent on the matter of the origin of this expression, usually classed as an Americanism, which means 'fine; marvelous; wonderful.' The only coherent theory available is offered by Mr. Frank E. Ferguson, of Lexington, Massachusetts:

> There is, I believe, some evidence that the term *hunky dory* came into use in the late 1850s; however, the dictionaries I have consulted all seem to provide no clear explanation of its origin. My wife, who lived many years in Japan, tells me that its "Japanese origin" is taken for granted there. The story is plausible, and perhaps even true. During the years following Admiral Perry's opening of Japan, many ships stopped in Japanese ports, and the sailors on shore leave trooped into the town and up into the surrounding hills looking for entertainment and perhaps companionship of sorts. The problem was how to return to the ship: having negotiated soberly the branching of narrow streets into narrower passages in the distant reaches on the outward trip, the return trip in an alcoholic fog was less certain. Nonetheless, once one reached the main street all was well, for that led straight to the wharf in many of the coastal towns, and Yokohama in particular. The street in question is, of course,

honcho dorii, or 'main street.' Wouldn't it be nice if this bit of etymology could be substantiated?

HUSHPUPPY

A 'deep-fried cornmeal fritter, usually spherical,' a term originating in the American South. The popular explanation for its origin is that such delectables, which are quickly made by a cook while engaged in more serious culinary pursuits, were tossed to quiet the ubiquitous dogs that whined for a handout at the kitchen door. They are quite delicious and are consumed by more people, one should think, than dogs. One might thus be tempted, in connection with a definition of *hushpuppy,* to recall Dr. Johnson's definition of oats: "A grain which in England is generally given to horses but in Scotland supports the people." It is rumored that it is in the canine purveyance of *hushpuppies* that etymologists would be well advised to seek the origin of the expression, *lucky dog.* Today, *hushpuppies* have spread to England but only because of the trade name for suede shoes made by Clarke.

HUSTLING DRAWERS

Underwear worn by female shoplifters, specially made for concealing their thefts.

I

ILL WIND (THAT BLOWS NOBODY GOOD)

The entire expression above is often shortened to *ill wind*. Its meaning, though metaphorical, is quite transparent. Its origin is probably nautical: there is every reason to expect an adverse wind to blow a vessel off course and, often, to disaster. The entertainer Danny Kaye, most of whose material was written by his wife, Sylvia Fine, sang a song in the 1940s in which the oboe was referred to as "an ill wind that nobody blows good."

INDIAN SUMMER

Etymologists have long pondered over the origin of this term, which describes the 'warm spell in late autumn that often follows the first frosts of winter in November, especially in New England.' A writer in 1804 suggested that its name probably came from the fact that its arrival was foretold to the early settlers by the Indians. In 1812, another commentator offered that it was so called after the belief by the Indians that the warmer days were brought by a wind from "the court of their great and benevolent God Cautantowwit, or the southwestern God." A somewhat fanciful theory (1823) attributed the warmth to the burning (by the Indians) of millions of acres of land, set to capture game. In 1824, a writer suggested that it was so called "because it afforded the Indians another opportunity of visiting the settlements with their destructive warfare." Evidence supporting one of these theories may one day emerge, but for the time being the available sources are silent on a credible, confirmable origin of the expression.

IN HOCK

This all-too-common Americanism, which means to 'have one's belongings in a pawn shop,' can be traced to the card game faro, in which the last card in the box was called the *hocketty card,* the card said to be *in hocketty* or *in hock.* When a player bet on a card that ended up *in hock* he was at a disadvantage, was himself *in hock,* and at risk of losing his bets. The transfer from gambling to more mundane financial situations is not farfetched, considering the prevalence of gambling in the Old West, whence the expression comes: the losing gambler may well have been forced to pawn possessions to pay his debts, taking a valuable to the hock shop for the readies.

(PASSENGER) IN THE CAPE ANN STAGE

As Cape Ann is a body of water in Massachusetts, there was no such coach as a Cape Ann Stage, and the expression is a jocular term for '(someone) rocking about in an advanced state of inebriation' (1856).

IN THE MONEY

Racetrack jargon for 'among the winning horses,' that is, first, second, or third. It also refers to a bettor whose horse finishes *in the money.*

IN THE SOUP

'In trouble or difficulty.' Although the source of this Americanism is generally conceded to be obscure, it seems likely that because it is equivalent to *in hot water,* the jocular transfer is transparent. *In hot water* may come from a humorous reference to the classic missionary, sitting in the cannibals' pot, ready to be cooked ('made into soup') and, presumably, eaten.

IVY LEAGUE

Quite literally, those colleges and universities of the northeastern United States having ivy-covered walls, namely, Harvard, Yale, Princeton, Columbia, Brown, Dartmouth, Cornell, and Pennsylvania. Figuratively, the ivy plant has long carried with it the connotation of age and venerability, though *Ivy League* is a relatively recent, twentieth-century term, more often used by those who attended those institutions than those who did not.

J

JAYWALKER

This common modern British English and American English term for a 'person who crosses a thoroughfare against the traffic lights' is said by most sources to be associated with the *jaybird*, known for its noisy, defiant ways. What the justification may be for such an analysis cannot be fathomed, for the word *jay* has been established in the language for at least a hundred years in the sense of 'fool, dupe, simpleton.' It seems probable that this sense, implying a 'stupid person from out of town, unfamiliar with traffic in the city (among other things),' yielded the *jay-* of *jaywalker*. This is likely to have been reinforced by (or may be a play on) *jayhawker,* an Americanism of unknown origin referring to a member of a guerrilla band in eastern Kansas in the 1850s and early 1860s known for pillaging as well as the conduct of irregular warfare. These notions of lawlessness and the sound of *jayhawker* seem likely to have produced *jaywalker*. The verb *jaywalk* is a back formation—that is, it was formed by the dropping of the *-er*.

JIM CROW

This term for the policies and practices of discrimination against Negroes and their resulting segregation is not heard as often today as formerly, but that is no indication that such attitudes and behavior have disappeared: only too pleased to **pass the buck** (*q.v.*), Americans now refer to (and deplore) that activity as characteristic of foreigners,

and it is now called *apartheid*. Although apartheid, properly (and appropriately) pronounced a-PART-hate, is transparent as to etymology—*apart* from French *à part* 'separate' + *-heit* the same as English *-hood* meaning 'state or condition'—Jim Crow does not yield so readily to historical interpretation. Its earliest evidence is seen in a Negro minstrel show song of the early nineteenth century (1830s), sung by a popular (white) entertainer of the day, Thomas D. Rice (1808–60):

> Come, listen all you gals and boys,
> I'se just from Tucky hoe;
> I'm goin' to sing a little song,
> My name's Jim Crow.
> CHORUS: Wheel about and turn about and do jis' so;
> Every time I wheel about I jump Jim Crow.

According to *The Negro Almanac* (Bellwether, 1976), at the rear of the Louisville theater was a livery stable, owned by a man named Crow, where worked a slave who called himself Jim Crow. This fellow was deformed and walked with an outrageous limp. Rice picked up the character as an object of ridicule, borrowing the song that Jim Crow was said to have sung habitually. Rice worked the song and lurching dance into his act and it at once became extraordinarily popular. "And so," goes the text of the *Almanac*, "Jim Crow, reinforcing the image of the black buffoon, jumped into the dramatic pantheon." *The History of Jim Crow,* an antislavery book, was published in England a few years after Rice's introduction of the Jim Crow character. In the context of today's atmosphere about racial prejudice, the old minstrel show may be viewed as having been anti-Negro; but for the hundred years during which such shows were staple entertainment—not only in America but abroad, as well—they were regarded (superficially, at least) merely as entertainment, though it is obvious that prejudice, underlying or overt, was fueled by such performances. It was more of a style of entertainment to performers like Al Jolson, who did his act in blackface, than a conscious act of denigration. And it came to an end only

recently, with the discontinuance of movie roles like those of Stepin Fetchit, Mantan Moreland (in Charlie Chan films), and the timorous Willie Best, because their characterizations proved offensive to blacks. Therefore, it is not easy to see how or why *Jim Crow* came to be singled out as a term epitomizing prejudice against blacks, especially since evidence that it originated among blacks is lacking. See also **Uncle Tom.**

JIMINY CRICKET

This popular creation of Walt Disney's had his origin with the Creator Himself—or with His son. It goes back to a time in America when Puritanism forbade—or at least inhibited—any utterance in which the Lord's name was taken in vain. Thus there sprang into being a number of what are called (in crossword puzzle clues, at any rate) "minced oaths," like *Gee whiz!* (and its elaboration, *Gee willikers!* or *willikens*), *Golly gee!*, and others, all a roundabout way of invoking Jesus Christ. Their manifestations are legion: *Gloryosky (Zero!)*, *Crimenentlies*, and so on. *Damned* became *darned; God damned* became *goldarned* or *goddam* or *goldinged; hell* became *heck*. Their variety seems endless: *Great Scott!*, *Great Caesar's ghost!*, *Good grief!* (for *Good God!*). Although some theorize that *Jiminy (Cricket)* comes from an attempt to invoke the twin Roman gods, the *Gemini*, such a call seems farfetched, partly because there is not much evidence of modern speakers' calling upon any Roman mythological figures, partly because evidence for using names of the most important deities is lacking (with the possible exception of *By Jove!*, which is probably a minced form of *By Jesus!*).

JUKE BOX

A coin-operated machine that offers a choice of musical records. *Juke boxes* were once situated in *juke joints*, which were disreputable places that people were wont to frequent for eating, drinking, dancing, and (originally) the indulgence of other fleshly pleasures. The word *juke*, spelled *jook* in earlier incarnations, has been traced to the fleshpots of New Orleans where it was an alternative for *the* four-letter word. In that sense, it has survived in some contexts in Caribbean English, but *juke,* in modern American English is not encountered out of combination, usually with *box*. Like *jazz,* which also carried a sexual denotation in its earlier existence, *juke* has lost all of its naughty meanings, having undergone what linguists call "amelioration."

K

KIT AND CABOODLE

There has been much speculation about the origin of this phrase, but—at least on the surface—its origins do not seem to be in the least obscure. The word *boodle,* traceable to Dutch *boedel* 'property, goods, effects,' is attested as early as 1699. In an extended sense, in the expression *the whole boodle,* it was popular during the nineteenth century, when it acquired a specialized meaning of 'money in general' which was then further specialized to 'counterfeit money or money obtained under false pretenses,' 'money used for bribery.' These latter usages gave rise to the word *boodleism* (or *boodlerism*) for the 'practice of bribing public officials.' Back to *the whole boodle,* it seems likely that *kit and . . .* could have been attached to it for emphasis. Where the *ca-* (or *ka-*) in *caboodle* came from is not certain, but there are other instances in the language in which meaningless syllables have been added to words for euphony or merely for fun (as in *kerplunk,* and the *k-* sound of *ca-* certainly goes well with that in *kit*). Thus, it seems quite possible that the progression went from *the whole boodle* to *the whole kit and boodle* to *the whole kit and caboodle.* If ample citations are not available for the transitional forms, that can easily be explained: of the writing of the nineteenth century that remains available (and thoroughly searched), little of it, relatively speaking, contained the slang of the day.

KNOCK INTO A COCKED HAT

In the late eighteenth century it was still the fashion for a man to wear a broad-brimmed hat with the brim turned up to the crown and there fastened, in two or three places, to form a bicorn or tricorn. Generally, the style was called a *cocked hat*. To those familiar with the alternative of leaving the brim flat and horizontal, it resembled a hat that might have been knocked askew in a skirmish. Thus, by a bit of shifting, *knock into a cocked hat* came to mean 'administer a sound thrashing.' Later, it was transferred to apply to anything, as a plan, or, as in this quotation from 1866, a place: "Although it took little more to knock Fort Sumter into a cocked hat. . . ." Vizetelly and de Bekker, in *A Desk-Book of Idioms and Idiomatic Phrases,* report that in the game of bowling, if the three pins remain standing at the angles of the triangle in which they are set up, the pattern was called a *cocked hat,* and the set was said to have been *knocked into a cocked hat.* Such a pattern is likely to foil most attempts at knocking down the rest of the pins, giving rise to another sense, to 'destroy one's plans' or 'deprive (anything) of its character.'

KNOW WHICH WAY THE CAT WILL JUMP

This folksy expression, meaning 'foretell the outcome of a situation,' is traced in Randolph and Wilson to the old custom of tossing a cat in a quilt at the end of a quilting party: the girl toward whom the cat jumps will be the first to marry.

L

LAME DUCK

This is an old expression, but its earlier meaning, '(any) incapacitated person,' was replaced by a specialized slang sense in the nineteenth century: 'one who is unable to meet his obligations on the stock exchange.' That sense has more recently been superseded by the modern political definition, 'an office holder who is completing his term and will not continue in that office in the next term.' Whether he or she will not hold the office again because of defeat in an election, because of resignation, by law, or for some other reason, that person is still a lame duck during the remainder of the term in office. The underlying sense of 'partly incapacitated' is carried through from the original, literal meaning.

LAY AN EGG

This common expression for 'fail utterly' is usually associated with the air-force phrase *lay an egg* 'drop a bomb.' In mainly theatrical contexts, in American English, *bomb* as a slang verb means 'fail,' and a *bomb* is a 'failure.' In British English, however, *bomb* means 'smashing success' as a noun, especially in the expression *It went like a bomb*. This etymology seems very unlikely, especially since *lay an egg* 'fail' appears to have preceded the bombing sense. Besides, the syntax is wrong: one does not *lay* a success or failure. It seems apparent that the *egg* referred to is, in British parlance, a *duck's egg*, or 'zero' (from its shape), which, for some reason that has never been satisfactorily explained (except by genuine perversity), is called a *goose egg* in American vernacular. Once the notion of 'failure' for *egg* is accepted, *lay an egg* 'fail' seems a rather obvious play on words.

LIFE IN THE FAST LANE
The *fast lane* is the lane on a multilane highway for accommodating the cars of those who feel compelled to travel at a greater speed than those content to cruise along within the speed limit. This relatively recent metaphor is usually applied to and by those 'young upwardly mobile professionals'—*yuppies*—who impatiently pursue (financial) success and try to give the impression that they are leaving the *squares* and other slowpokes behind.

LIVE TALLY
To 'live together without being married'—said originally of a man and woman surviving together as man and wife, but applicable, one supposes, to any sort of combination of two people in a similar situation. This English expression has been in the language for several hundred years, and one is given to wonder why confusing concoctions like *POSSLQ, alternative other,* etc., need have been created. Either partner in such an enterprise is called a *tally,* which is convenient. *Leman* is another old term for 'lover' or 'mistress.'

LIVE WITH THE WORLD
Often found in negative contexts, this American ruralism refers to being 'in touch with what is going on,' as in *Don' know but what Jane's out of it—she jus' don' live with the world no more.*

LOCOFOCO
Originally the nickname, later an official name of the Equal Rights party, a faction of the Democratic party in New York State. It also came to be used (before 1850) to refer to the entire Democratic party. As reported in the *DAE,* quoting an 1888 source, "The term was applied to the

radical wing of the Democratic party, way back in the Jacksonian days, because of a circumstance that occurred at a Democratic meeting in Tammany Hall [in New York City] in 1834. The discussion having become very warm, the President put out the gas for the purpose of breaking up the meeting, but one of the extremists produced some friction matches, then just coming into use under the name of *loco-foco* matches, and relighted the gas, when order was restored and the meeting duly held."

LUNCH-HOOK
See **corn-stealer**.

M

MAKE ONE'S POINT

Meaning to 'establish one's argument' (though not, necessarily, convincingly), *make one's point* comes from crapshooting.

MAN ON THE HORSE

A late nineteenth-century expression for the 'man in authority.' In this form, it is first encountered in a British publication, the *Pall Mall Gazette* of 1887, in which it is referred to as a "picturesque American phrase." It is probably connected with the earlier (1879) *man on horseback*, used originally in reference to General Ulysses S. Grant but later extended to others in authority, especially when they were presented or perceived as knights in shining armor.

MARBLEHEAD TURKEY

See **Cape Cod turkey**.

MICHIGAN BANKROLL

A gambler's term for a roll of bills consisting mainly of plain paper or one-dollar notes with a few of larger denomination on the outside.

MIND YOUR P'S AND Q'S

Not all etymologies have to be obscure, convoluted, or reliant on an understanding of the arcana of linguistics. This exhortation, urging that care be taken to behave prop-

erly in all respects, seems a straightforward enough rec-
ommendation to schoolchildren to ensure that the tails
(descenders) of the letters *p* and *q* are on the proper side
and not to write one for the other. Left to their own devices, imaginative quasi-etymologists have set forth the
curious notion that the expression comes from French *pies
et queues—pies* as in 'peacoat' and *queues* for 'tails,' in reference to the tails on the letters. More likely, *pies et queues*
is a bit of French word-play on *p et q*, referring to the
letters (as in English), with the names of the letters in
French being pronounced "pay" and "kuh" (as in French
peu). Despite all this, there is nothing in the evidence citing
the phrase that it has a French source. Another pundit
would have it that the caution is offered by a publican
whose customer is coming close to his credit limit: *mind
your p's* (for 'pints') *and q's* (for 'quarts'). When quarts of
any beverage were served up in a public house cannot be
determined, nor, for that matter, when the permission to
drink on credit was sufficiently prevalent to have given
birth to a cliché. It seems, from evidence in the *OED*, that
at least two expressions, one cautioning people to distin-
guish between the letters *p* and *q*, the other having some
vague connection with *pints* and *quarts,* were current during
part of the nineteenth century, so any analysis may not be
as clear-cut as might be wished.

MONDAY-MORNING QUARTERBACK

This Americanism refers to an 'armchair strategist who
works out on Monday, often at tiresome length, the tactics
that should have been used by the quarterback—that is,
the player who calls the plays in American football—in
the game that was played on Sunday afternoon.' The
expression has overtones of criticism for the game as played,
but it more often connotes the advantages of hindsight
over the exigencies that dictate the decisions of the moment. It frequently refers to the activity, rather than the
person, in the verbal noun form, *Monday-morning quarter-
backing*.

MR. CLEAN

'Someone—invariably a male, usually a politician—who is upstanding and honest and whose reputation is unsullied by any taint of scandal or wrongdoing.' The expression entered the language in the 1960s, when a household cleaning liquid was commercially introduced in America and widely advertised on television using a bald, muscular, middle-aged model who was "Mr. Clean." The practice of referring to an individual who is the epitome of some characteristic or is closely associated with a certain activity as "Mr. ———" is ancient in the language: the word *mister* comes from *master,* which was originally the designation used to identify a man with his *métier* (another word in the same etymological family). Thus, in modern times, we have had *Mr. 880,* the nickname of a kindly, elderly forger who made his own crude one-dollar bills, evidently to provide pocket money to buy sweets for neighborhood children. All of the bills bore the same serial number, which ended in 880, hence the sobriquet. As with *Mr. Clean,* the word used is often an adjective: *Mr. Big.* The name of the prime minister of Burma in the 1950s and '60s, *U Nu,* means 'Mr. Clean' in Burmese.

MUGWUMP

Although there is a facetious etymology for *mugwump*— "a fence sitter; one who sits on the fence with his mug on one side and his wump on the other"—the true origin is traceable to an Algonquian word *mogkiomp* 'important or great man; big chief.' It was first applied by Charles A. Dana, editor of *The New York Sun* (1884), during the (unsuccessful) presidential campaign of Republican James G. Blaine against Democrat Grover Cleveland. Dana's reference was to the indecisive Republicans who failed to support Blaine (and, presumably, lost him the election). In Britain, *mugwump* is used to refer to 'any cockalorum, or self-important man, who behaves pompously.'

N

NAME NAMES

To *name names* is to 'identify people by their names'; it is commonly used in adverse contexts, as in the case of a culprit revealing his accomplices' names or an investigator specifying the names of those involved in some wrongdoing. Although the expression has the ring of a modern idiom, citations for it (or for examples that are so close as to be semantically indistinguishable from it) can be found as early as the fourteenth century, in Wycliffe's writings: "Each man that nameth the name of the Lord." This citation carries no shady taint, of course, for that connotation did not arise till later. A quotation from Defoe (1715) is found in the *OED:* "It is a . . . profane thing to name his name on slight occasions."

NICKEL AND DIME (SOMEONE) TO DEATH

This Americanism is used metaphorically to mean to 'harass with niggling matters when more important issues are at stake.' Its origins are too obvious to recount, but it has other, literal applications as well, in which the sense is to

'erode one's resources by petty bills for trifling goods or services.'

NORFOLK HOWARD

This idiom is a British slang euphemism for a 'bedbug,' otherwise known by any number of aliases, like *scarlet creeper, crimson rambler,* etc. According to the *OED* the bedbug acquired its proper-sounding name when an advertisement appeared in *The Times* of June 26, 1862 announcing that one *Joshua Bug* had changed his name to *Norfolk Howard.* This must surely rank among the collector's items for connoisseurs of etymological originality.

NOT KNOW BEANS ABOUT (SOMETHING)

To 'be ignorant or stupid,' this common expression may have come from a rural American saying, *not know beans when the poke* [bag] *is open,* in other words, 'not be able to identify something as ordinary as beans when looking right at them.'

OFF THE WALL

This phrase, which may be applied to a person, plan, idea, or other suitable object, means 'crazy, mad, harebrained.' A recent (post-World War II) expression, it is probably related to *go* or *crawl up the wall,* which is what insane or very agitated people are said to do when they lose all control. Once up there, what they are likely to produce is a thoroughly mad idea or scheme, while exhibiting totally irrational behavior. Of course, all of these notions are characterized as hyperbolic, or grossly exaggerated.

O.K., OKEH, OKAY

Few terms in any language have had so much attention paid to them as *O.K.* and its variants. Reams have been written on the subject, and the etymology has aroused the interest of a large number of amateurs. A letter to *The Times* (September 10, 1980) set forth the suggestion that it is an "Anglicization of the word for 'good' in Ewe, the West African language spoken by many of the slaves taken to the southern states." Logical as this may seem, there is no supporting evidence for it. In a reply to that letter, Robert W. Burchfield, Chief Editor of the *Oxford English Dictionaries,* summed up the evidence, much of which has been gathered and explicated by Professor Allen Walker Read, the prominent American linguist. According to Read, *O.K.* first was used as a facetious variant of the initial letters of 'oll korrect' ('all correct'), in 1839. In 1840, because of its association and possibly also because it was already fast acquiring its modern sense of general approval, it was picked up as a nickname and slogan for Martin Van Buren, the Democratic candidate for the presidency. Van Buren was born in Kinderhook, New York, and *O.K.* fitted in very nicely with *Old Kinderhook,* his nickname. In the century and a half since, *O.K.*—as an adjective, noun, verb, sentence substitute, what have you—has become universal, has been adopted into virtually every language on earth, and has become one of the most common terms in many of them.

OLD STAMPING-GROUND

A *stamping-ground* was 'any place to which animals habitually returned,' and its use is attested in American sources of the late nineteenth century. In a transferred sense, it came to mean 'any place to which a person returned after some interval,' particularly with the connotation that such a place was a familiar one where the person had been reared, had experienced good times, had exercised some influence—or "all of the above." It is more frequently than not preceded by *old,* partly in the sense of 'former,' partly conveying affection born of familiarity.

ONCE IN A BLUE MOON

'Rarely,' is the meaning. According to E. Cobham Brewer, in *The Dictionary of Phrase & Fable,* the moon was blue on December 10, 1883. Another commentator points to the eruption of the Javanese island, Krakatoa, in 1883, and the stratospheric volcanic ash that colored the sunsets for some time afterward as the possible cause of the moon's bluish appearance.

ON ONE'S BEAM ENDS

This phrase, which means 'in a precarious or hazardous situation,' is, like many others, nautical in origin. In a wooden vessel, the beams are the horizontal timbers that run at right angles to the keel—athwartships, as they say in nautical contexts—and support the deck. Thus, the ends of the beams meet the hull at the sides, above the waterline.

If a ship or boat is careened (heeled) over far enough—
that is, on her beam ends—she can founder from the water
pouring in over the rail to the area below decks and is,
consequently, in a dangerous position.

ON ONE'S HIGH HORSE

As readers of early romances (before Women's Lib) will
recall, knights, kings, and other V.I.P.s rode chargers while
their ladies trailed along, borne on palfreys, which are
ordinary, small saddle horses. The larger horses were needed
to carry the heavy armor and other battle paraphernalia of
contemporary heroes, the little horses being adequate for
the support of the delicate members of the species sporting
their wimples. Clergymen and others from the lower castes
of society at the time were also carried by less imposing
mounts, allowing the haughty to look down upon them
from their "high horses."

ON THE CUFF, OFF THE CUFF

At the turn of the century and well into the 1920s, men
wore shirts with stiffly starched collars and cuffs, which
were removable: it was not till later on that attached collars
and cuffs, formerly on work clothes only, became standard
attire. Those who could not afford starched cotton collars
and cuffs wore them made out of Celluloid, which could
be wiped clean easily. Men got into the habit of penciling
notations on their cuffs, which became convenient portable
memo pads. A typical use among shopkeepers was to note
accounts or debts, and, if one charged a purchase in a shop
where his credit was good, he asked to have the transaction
put *on the cuff*. Thus, the original sense of the phrase was
'on credit.' Later, either because such accounts were dif-

ficult to collect, because collection dragged on for a long time, or merely as a joke, *on the cuff* acquired the meaning 'free; on the house,' which is its predominant sense today.

Accounts were not the only information noted on cuffs in those days: they were used for all sorts of memoranda. If someone were giving a speech he would often jot down some of the key points he wished to make and refer to them during the delivery. This practice was not followed by those who made formal speeches, which were fully written out or memorized; but extemporaneous remarks were delivered *off the cuff,* an expression that is current today meaning 'informal, casual' despite the virtual disappearance of stiff cuffs from the male wardrobe.

THE OTHER END OF THE AVENUE
'The White House or the Capitol,' which are at opposite ends of Pennsylvania Avenue, in Washington, D.C. (1903).

P

PAINT THE TOWN RED

The origin of this common expression is undocumented, and various guesses have been advanced. Today, it means to 'go on a spree'; a hundred years ago, it carried the connotation of destruction, sometimes through the setting of fires, sometimes accompanied by bloody encounters. Whether the idiom owes its origins to violence or, as another theorist would have it, to the fact that red is regarded as an extreme (owing to its position in the spectrum) is anybody's guess. This latter suggestion no doubt stems from the facetious quotation from the *Boston Journal,* September 13, 1884: "A 'spectrophotometric study of pigments,' by Professor Nicolls, is recommended to young men who intend to 'paint the town red.'"

PALM OFF

Victims of the unscrupulous who have given them something of lesser value (or of no value) in exchange for money or who have otherwise defrauded them have had something *palmed off* on them. The expression comes from those who practice legerdemain, those who know how to show a dupe a valuable, then *palm* it and substitute something of lesser value. The expression has been extended to mean 'persuade someone to accept in exchange for value anything he may not even want': *The dealer tried to palm off that old jalopy on me, but I don't even know how to drive.*

PASS THE BUCK

Dictionaries list quite a number of different homographs—that is, words spelled identically but having different etymologies—for *buck,* from the 'male of any of several animals' to 'completely,' as in *buck naked.* According to tradition, the *buck* in *pass the buck* is short for a 'knife with a buckhorn handle,' described as a common object used in poker to indicate the dealer's position or, by putting it into the pot, to remind "the winner that he has some privilege or duty when his turn to deal next comes," according to *The Random House Unabridged Dictionary.* The *OED Supplement* shows a similar treatment. The meaning of this common idiom is to 'foist responsibility on someone else.' It has given rise to a verb, *buck,* which merely means to 'send something to someone else' and is often used as a synonym for 'pass around'; thus, in an office environment, one might say, "Mrs. Goodwin, please buck this memo to all department heads." (This everyday sense is missing from most dictionaries.) In the mid-1940s, President Harry S. Truman coined the expression, *the buck stops here,* meaning that after everyone else had busily passed on responsibility to someone else, the ultimate accountability came to rest on the President's desk. Both expressions enjoy—if that is the right word—popularity wherever English is spoken.

PEANUT GALLERY

Some commentators derive the figurative sense of this American English phrase, 'any insignificant source' (usually of comment), from a literal interpretation: those who sat in the (upper) gallery of a theater, in the cheapest seats, (usually) ate peanuts (or popcorn) during a performance.

This seems unnecessarily labored, for *peanut* has long carried with it the sense of 'pettiness, cheapness, insignificance,' (as in "He works for peanuts"), and *gallery* is well established as a place whence issued approval or disapproval associated with the baser tastes. This can be seen in *play to the gallery*, which means 'perform for the pleasure of those with little taste or discernment.' Thus, *peanut* can be viewed merely as a reinforcement for *gallery*, possibly at a time (in American English) when *gallery*, no longer much used as a term for a section of a theater, had lost much of its stigma. The term *peanut politics*, an Americanism dating from the late nineteenth century, referred to politics conducted in an "underhand" (that is, "underground"), not a petty fashion.

PECULIAR INSTITUTION
This obsolete euphemism, from the late 1700s, was used in reference to slavery.

PELL-MELL
There was an old French game, *pelle-melle*, which consisted of a player's attempt to strike a ball so that it would pass through a hoop hung at the end of an alley. It was probably based on a sport originally played on horseback. It became popular in England, and a course was established near St. James's Palace, London, for the use of the nobility. The site of that playing field is now called *Pall Mall* and is the center of "Clubland" in London. *Pell-mell* being an active game, its name came to be used metaphorically for 'any frenzied activity involving a great deal of rushing to and fro.'

PHILADELPHIA LAWYER
This expression is somewhat contradictory, for one of its applications is to a 'shrewd, nit-picking attorney' while the other—perhaps in admiration of such attributes in the profession—is to a 'lawyer who displays great ability.' One source traces its origins to a reference to an Andrew Hamilton, a lawyer from Philadelphia, who in 1735 successfully

defended John Peter Zenger in a libel action brought against him for something published in his newspaper. As the evidence appeared to be overwhelmingly against Zenger, winning his case was a major coup, which, not incidentally, helped establish in the New World the principle of freedom of the press. These facts about Zenger are well documented. The problem arises because the first citation we have is from 1803 (*OED*), and it seems highly unlikely that such an expression would have emerged only after a seventy-year gestation period. On the other hand, two important facts must be emphasized: first, our 1803 citation is merely the earliest evidence found and not necessarily the first time the expression appeared in print; and second, one cannot assume that the first time something appears in print is the first time it was used: it might have been—indeed, probably was—used orally for many years before being enshrined in written form. Thus, citational evidence can be used only as a guide, for, as historical lexicographers are only too well aware, any citation they may find can often be antedated. How *Philadelphia lawyer*—or, for that matter, any word or expression—may figure in all this is not easy to determine; but it can be said with reasonable confidence that its connotation is largely pejorative today, and its original association with Hamilton and Zenger would seem to be tenuous in the absence of solid, contemporary evidence.

PIG LATIN, DOG LATIN

This jocular term refers to "phoney" Latin, or macaronics, that is, 'English words to which Latin endings have been applied to make them appear erudite.' *Pig Latin* is the usual American form; *Dog Latin*—the term is related to *doggerel*—seems to be the more popular term in England but is also used in the U.S. An example is the principal parts of the verb "skato": *skato, slippere, falli, bumptum.* The earliest citation offered by the *OED* for *Dog Latin* is from 1770, and the origin is described as attributable to the general use of *dog* (or *dog's*) in the sense of 'barbarous, bad.' The same notion of something of low quality is seen in the expressions *going to the dogs, dog's lunch* or *breakfast*, and other uses of *dog* and *cur.*

Pig Latin is also the name given to the children's language game, used as a kind of secret code, in which the first sound of a word or compound is placed at the end followed by the sound *-ay.* Thus, *Pig Latin* would be pronounced *igpay atinlay, hushpuppy* as *ushpay uppypay.* A variation of this is *Openglopish,* in which the syllable *-op-* is pronounced before each vowel in a word (*Openglopish* being *Openglopish* for *English*), as in *Popig Lopatopin* for *Pig Latin.*

PIN (SOMEONE'S) EARS BACK

Curiously, this common threat of violence is documented only in the *OED Supplement,* where it is defined but not given any provenance. It seems likely to come from the practice of pinning a horse's ears—that is, tying them with a cord which can be twisted by means of a stick in order to better control a recalcitrant animal. (Twitching, in which a cord is tied round the nose and upper lip of a refractory horse, is more commonly done these days, especially in the northeastern United States.) If that is the source, it is probably from the southwestern U.S., where it is considered a severe method and is used only on wild horses.

PISS ON ICE

This is a somewhat old-fashioned (1920s?) Americanism meaning the same as to *live high off the hog,* or to 'have plenty of money to spend.' It derives from the practice, in posh restaurants and nightclubs, of placing a block of ice into the urinals in men's rooms in order to stanch the odor. As such a use of ice was something of an extravagance, those who *pissed on ice* were those who could afford to frequent the luxurious retreats.

PLAY FOOTSIE

This phrase, of recent coinage, has two literal meanings, either to 'flirt by clandestinely touching or stroking another's foot with one's own (as under a table, while others are about)' or to 'exchange information dishonestly with another player, as at cards, by signaling with one's foot under the table.' Either or both of these could have given rise to the much more common metaphorical sense, to 'enter into a secret, usually questionable relationship together, especially with an exchange of favors.' Thus, an informer could be said to *play footsie* with the police, a shady businessman with a politician who might influence an increase in his profits, and so on. The implication is usually one of treachery, but not on a major scale; it sometimes carries the connotation of tentativeness, as in the case of one party seeking such a relationship and, in this sense, carries over the earlier notion of flirtation.

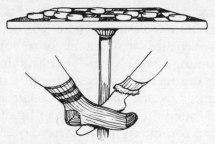

PLAY HARDBALL

Hardball is ordinary baseball, as contrasted with *softball,* a version of the game played by nonprofessional (local) men's and women's clubs and by professional women ballplayers with a larger, softer ball adopted because it cannot be hit as far and can therefore be played on a smaller field. The rules differ somewhat, but the import of the expression, *play hardball,* is to 'be engaged seriously in something; not be simply "playing" a game, but engaging in it earnestly.'

PLAY HOOKEY or HOOKY

The origin of this familiar American English idiom, which appears in British English and which means to 'play the truant from school,' has not been satisfactorily explained. The possible etymologies include: (1) *hookey* as a variant of *hockey,* suggesting that truants played that game with sufficient frequency to be associated with it; (2) *hookey,*

derived in schoolboy fashion from *hook it* 'depart; run off
or away.' The first seems unlikely because hockey was
traditionally played only at schools; the second is a bit
remote but would seem more likely if some intermediate
evidence is forthcoming.

PREACHER'S SEAT

A posture in which the bottom is down and the head and
feet are up, as a kid might assume when jumping into the
old swimming hole, especially in Missouri: *do the preacher's
seat* is the expression commonly employed.

PROCTER & GAMBLE

Narcotics addicts' euphemistic slang for *paregoric* (also called
P.G., from "Para Goric"), a tincture of opium containing
camphor, formerly a common medication, especially for
children, to check diarrhea and having the added advantage
(from the parents' point of view) of making a child drowsy.
Addicts refine it by evaporating off the camphor and al-
cohol by chilling it (to solidify the camphor) or by boiling
it off; they then drink it or inject it directly into a vein.
The association between P.G. and Procter & Gamble, the
large U.S. corporation, is self-evident.

PROFESSOR OF DUST AND ASHES

This jocular epithet was applied by college students to the
person charged with the care and cleaning of their quarters
(1847).

PUT ON (THE) DOG

Some measure of mystery surrounds the origin of this
idiom, which is not attested earlier than the beginning of
the twentieth century. Its meaning is well enough understood—to 'affect sophistication; behave pretentiously'—
but the problem arises when one examines the enormous
number of citations (as in the *OED*) for *dog*: virtually all
of them show that *dog* is invariably the epitome of denigration. 'Something bad' is a *dog; going to the dogs* means

'getting worse'; a *dog in the manger* is a 'cowering cur'; an 'ugly person' is a *dog,* and so on. Whence, then, comes the "uplifting" sense of *dog* in *put on (the) dog?* The answer is not readily forthcoming, though a suggestion may be found in the obsolete idiom to *be (old) dog at,* a British English phrase not attested since the middle of the eighteenth century, when it meant to 'exhibit experience or knowledge.' It may be related to the (negative) *you can't teach an old dog new tricks,* in the (positive) sense that an "old dog already knows the (old) tricks." Thus, while *put on (the) dog* may be a far cry from these other expressions in form, the semantic connection may be there, even though the earliest quotation for it in the *OED* dates from 1915.

PUT ONE'S FOOT IN IT

This common idiom has two meanings: (1) 'say (or, sometimes, do) something impolitic, undiplomatic, or just plain wrong and get into trouble as a result'; (2) 'ruin or spoil something; burn food when cooking it.' The first is short for *open one's mouth and put one's foot in it,* which, although it evokes an image of awkwardness, is not readily traced to any literal activity—at least, such an act is not sufficiently well attested for linguists to accept it as meaningful in determining the origin. The second sense, however, is an old English expression, explained by this quotation from William Tyndale's *Works* (1530s):

> If the porage be burned to, or the meate ouer rosted, we say the bishop hath put his foote in the potte or the bishop hath played the cooke, because the bishops burn . . . whosoever displeaseth them.

PUT THE KIBOSH ON (SOMETHING)

This common expression, meaning to 'ruin; bring to an (ignominious) end; destroy the plans for,' has a long and curious history in the language. Usually pronounced KYE-bosh, the pronunciation kaBOSH is sometimes heard, especially in England; the spelling variants *kybosh* and *kye-*

bosh are also noted. The fullest description is given in the Supplement to the *Century Dictionary,* in which it is suggested that the *ki-, kye-,* or *ky-* part is related to the *ker-* of *kerplunk* and other, similar words, while the *bosh* is associated with a word of Turkish origin meaning, as it does in English, 'stuff and nonsense.' *Century* further comments on the word *kibosh* as having no specific meaning— something like 'thingamabob, dingus,' etc. This latter point is certainly not the case today, when *kibosh* appears only in the idiom, which has a very specific, identifiable meaning. As to the former point, it seems unlikely that the word would have gained stress on the first syllable had its origin been from the *ker-* of *kerplunk,* for such words are not so stressed, the *ker-* being a sort of a "windup" syllable. A very similar form, *kye-bosk,* appears in Dickens's *Sketches by "Boz."* Earlier uses seem to have been more closely associated with the sense of 'put the finishing touches on,' with no adverse connotation discernible. Other uses, for *kibosh* alone, show a range of meanings from 'something indefinite,' to the 'real thing,' to 'Portland cement,' to 'substance used for filling cracks or for other purposes in the finishing of architectural sculptures,' to 'wages, money' (this from Cornwall), to 'affectation, display.' The *Century Dictionary* also cites a verb, *kibosh,* meaning to 'squash completely, terminate' and to "throw Portland cement on (carved stonework) with a blowpipe and a brush so as to enhance the shadows." Recent theory, expressed in the *OED Supplement,* is that the word may come from Yiddish. In *A Dictionary of Slang and Unconventional English* (8th edition, 1984), the current editor, Paul Beale, presents a good summary of the theories about the origin of *kibosh,* among them, recording that Eric Partridge had evidence that *kye* is from Yiddish 'eighteen,' *bosh* a slang word for 'pence.' "If this is correct," Beale writes, "it may be that this arbitrary sum is the answer. . . . The '18' crops up again [in later reference to] a prison sentence of 18 months." Sol Steinmetz, an expert in Yiddish, points out (*Yiddish and English,* University of Alabama Press, 1986) that the

word *chai,* made up of the letters *khet* ('eight' + *yod* 'ten,')
means 'alive, living.' One is given to wonder whether a
life sentence was, at some time, somewhere, commuted
to eighteen years, which would provide a double reference.
Today, *chai* is used by Jews as a basic unit of almsgiving
(eighteen dollars). Finally, there is the word *caboche,* from
French, used in heraldic descriptions of an animal, especially a deer, beheaded just behind the antlers. The feasibility of associating beheading with the effective ruination
of an animal, later extended to anything, seems eminently
acceptable.

R

RAINBOW or CHRISTMAS ROLL
Narcotics addicts' slang for an 'assortment of barbiturates,' reported in Maurer; so called because of the multicolored capsules.

RAIN PITCHFORKS
Originally, this expression was used (1815 ff.) to express the notion of improbability; but, unlike most words and phrases, which change from literal meaning to figurative, this one seems to have lost its earlier figurative sense and is today used as a hyperbole meaning to 'rain very hard': *It rained pitchforks last night.*

RARING TO GO
The spelling of this expression is questionable: those who think of it as a contraction for *rearing* or *roaring* spell it *r'aring,* or because the final *-g* is almost never pronounced, *r'arin'.* Semantically, either *rearing* or *roaring* fits: the former in the sense of an eager horse, forelegs pawing the air as when fighting to go forward against the pressure of the bit; the latter in the sense of a person making a lionlike noise as a release for frustrated, pent-up energy. In any event, the meaning of *raring to go* is 'extremely eager to begin something.'

RAT RACE
Anyone who has seen a group of rats running along a narrow, confined way can easily conjure up the literal image

of frenzied activity, with the rodents climbing over one another and running along others' backs. That is the source of this metaphor, which is usually applied to the frenetic competitiveness encountered in the conduct of business, especially in a large city crowded with others who are trying to get ahead.

REDSTICK
An 'Indian hostile to the United States.' Tecumseh (1768?–1813), the Indian chief, carried with him a red stick to which were ascribed magical properties; those who sided with him and joined his war party were originally called *Redsticks*. Later on, the term was applied to any hostile Indian, whether associated with Tecumseh or not; the term has not been in use since the mid 1800s.

RIGHT SMART
An Ozarkism, this phrase has nothing to do with cleverness; it means 'large amount or distance'; it indicates a mass, not a numerable quantity. Thus, one might say *It's a right smart piece to town* or comment that he had sold *a right smart of corn*.

RING FINGER
Every youngster (and some adults) can easily be confused by the fact that people have five fingers on each hand till one starts counting them, when, for some unknown reason, it is abruptly decided that there are four fingers and a thumb. Thus, the third finger is the one next to the little finger: it ought to be the fourth finger, but that is not an issue to argue here. This finger is so called from Roman

times: steeped—quite naturally—in the anatomy of romance (or the romance of anatomy—or romantic anatomy), the Romans thought that a nerve from the fourth finger led directly to the heart and that a ring on that finger, exchanged with one's beloved, established a heart-to-heart connection.

ROOT HOG OR DIE

An early nineteenth-century expression urging the necessity of working hard or suffering the undesirable consequences. A quotation from 1866 yields a good sense: "It has been a common practice with farmers . . . to raise [hogs] upon the principle of 'root hog or die.' That is, to turn them out in to the woods or on to the prairies to get their own living." *Root hog* is not in the current idiom of English, and it seems to be an exhortation addressed to a hog, though it is not attested with commas: that is, there are no examples found in the form "Root, hog, or die!" That is possibly because, by the time the expression first appeared in print (1834), it was already a cliché in the language.

RUBBERNECK

This somewhat old-fashioned term for 'tourist' has suffered a revival over the past dozen years, though in a slightly transferred sense. At the turn of the century (and later), it sprang up in New York, where it referred to the goggle-eyed rubes who went to the Big City, craning their necks in all directions to take in the sights. A common attributive use in those days was in *rubberneck bus, rubberneck tour,* etc. The word died out during the 1930s but was revived with the recent creation of the traffic reporter, that helicopter-borne radio broadcaster who warns listeners away from congested thoroughfares during morning and evening rush hours in some of the larger American cities. If there is a car crash or other road accident or breakdown, motorists traveling on the opposite (unobstructed) side of the road invariably slow down to view the carnage, satisfying their morbid curiosity and causing what traffic reporters delight in calling *rubberneck* (or *rubbernecking*) *delays.*

RUBE GOLDBERG

Reuben Lucius Goldberg (1883–1970) was a popular American cartoonist famous for his drawings of outlandishly complex contraptions contrived to perform relatively simple tasks. They involved not only exaggeratedly elaborate mechanical devices but midgets, trained animals, etc. He might, for example, have a headache-cure machine with a small boy who opens his mouth to receive a piece of chocolate which is released at the press of a button; the boy's lower jaw is attached to a string which, pulled when he opens his mouth, rings a bell that awakens a sleeping woman who immediately arises to brush her teeth; the action of her arm, which is attached to a saw, cuts through a plant on which an acrobat is standing; he falls onto a teeter to the other end of which is fastened a cup containing an aspirin tablet; the aspirin tablet is catapulted through the air and into the open mouth of the person with the headache (who pressed the button). Such a contrivance came to be called a *Rube Goldberg machine* or just a *Rube Goldberg,* and the name came to be applied to any device or system that is infinitely more complicated than it needs to be to do its job.

RUB OUT

According to J. L. Dillard, this idiom, meaning to 'kill' (by 'erasing from the face of the earth'?) might be traceable to Plains Indian sign language in which *kill* is signed by "a kind of rubbing motion." In any event, the notion that it comes from 1920s gangster lingo, as posited by H. L. Mencken, is easily confuted by citations that reach well back into the nineteenth century.

RUN AMOK

This hybrid expression—ordinary English *run* plus Malay *amoq*—is usually encountered with the meaning to 'behave in a wild, uncontrolled manner.' Considering its Malaysian origin, that puts it mildly, for *moq* in Malay refers to a man—women do not seem to have had equal rights in southeast Asia—who has been suddenly possessed by a fit of insanity that causes him to dash about crazily, kris in hand, chopping away at all those he meets, either killing them or doing them grievous bodily damage. Those who have written about the phenomenon, linguists and anthropologists, are not entirely clear as to whether the affliction is genetic among Malays or a culturally acquired proclivity to wreak occasional havoc. As most of those suffering from it are killed before they can do too much damage, useful clinical information is lacking. It seems safe to say, however, that Western men are seized by fits of murderous frenzy from time to time as well—witness snipers who kill innocent people, for instance—so the affliction does not seem to be confined to Malaya, where it has scarcely been a common occurrence. A variant spelling is *amuck*.

RUN THE GAUNTLET

The word *gauntlet* is a spelling error for *gantlet* and has nothing whatsoever to do with gloves. *Gantlet* goes back to Swedish *gatlopp* from the words meaning 'gate' and 'leap.' The activity described was, literally, the forcing of a man to run between two lines of men who beat him with sticks and whips as a form of punishment. Today, the phrase is (fortunately) used metaphorically, as in referring to a new play, which must *run the gauntlet* of the Broadway critics.

RUSSIAN ROULETTE

A "game"—that is, perverse activity that consists of loading one cartridge into a revolver, spinning the chamber, holding the muzzle to one's own temple, and pulling the trigger. It is some sort of colossal black joke, "played" only by fools (who, needless to say, must "lose" if they engage in it long enough). Its name, too, is a joke, a satiric comment on the rash toughness for which Russian soldiers became known during World War II; there is no evidence that they played it. However, there is evidence that some fatalities have occurred from it, possibly an example of death imitating art.

S

SECOND STRING

The source of this familiar idiom is another frequently heard expression, to *have two strings to one's bow,* in which *bow* is used in the archery, not the musical-instrument sense. One who has two strings to his bow is one who has something to fall back on, who has an alternative resource. The *second string* is the name for the resource, now usually applied to an auxiliary roster of players in a sport. Because of this, it sometimes carries a denigrating connotation, like *second class,* leaving *first string* to be applied to regular team players.

SECURITY BLANKET

This metaphor for 'anything that brings solace and comfort' has its origin in the comic strip *Peanuts,* by Charles Schulz, which began in the 1950s and has become one of the most widely syndicated features of all time. In it, a small boy, Linus, is characteristically depicted as sucking his thumb and clutching a baby blanket, from which he is separated only with the greatest distress.

SEE THE ELEPHANT

" 'That's sufficient,' as Tom Haynes said when he saw the elephant." This is a quotation from 1840 that appears in the *OED*. It must be remembered that elephants were rare and wonderful beasts to Europeans and Americans in those days—so wonderful as to seem almost imaginary. Those who had actually seen an elephant were of the opinion that "Now we have seen everything!" so unusual a sight was the animal. Thus, the expression *to have seen the elephant* came to mean 'to have experienced what things (and life) are like, especially in a big city.' The *OED* quotation is interesting for another reason: it refers to "Tom Haynes," who might have been a specific person but, more likely, was the semifictional Haynes (or Hanes) who figured in an expression popular at the time, *My name is Hanes,* a cliché with no particular meaning that was uttered by a person who was about to leave a place or gathering. According to a piece by Gerald Cohen, published in *Verbatim* (VI, 1), the article describing the incident that gave rise to the origin of the phrase appeared in the newspaper *Evening Star* (date unknown) and was reprinted in *The Subterranean* (November 15, 1845), a New York newspaper. According to the story, a Mr. Hanes [*sic*—no given name is mentioned] was riding along near President Thomas Jefferson's home in Virginia and by chance encountered the president, who was also on horseback. Hanes was a Federalist, bitterly opposed to Jefferson and his administration; striking up a conversation, Hanes immediately began to vilify Jefferson—whom he did not recognize—and continued to carry on a diatribe against him and his policies. Jefferson remained quiet. They finally arrived at Jefferson's residence, and Hanes was cordially invited to come in for some refreshment. As he was alighting, Hanes asked his companion's name, as the report goes:

"Jefferson," said the President.

"What! Thomas Jefferson?"

"Yes, sir. Thomas Jefferson."

"President Thomas Jefferson?" continued the astounded Federalist.

"The same," rejoined Mr. Jefferson.

"Well, my name is Hanes!" and putting spurs to his horse, he was out of hearing instantly. There is no reason to assume that this Hanes and the Haynes referred to in the citation are one and the same, but it makes a good story. . . .

SHAMBLES, IN A

The earliest recordings of this word, traced to the Old English of the tenth century in the *OED,* show its use to have been figurative for a 'stool,' especially a 'kitchen stool.' It is probably related to *scamble* 'low kitchen bench' and to other words beginning with the *sk-* (also spelled *sc-*) and *sh-* sounds. The connections, however, both in form and in meaning, are not always evident. As other observers have pointed out, either because of the high frequency of certain words beginning with *sk-* or *sh-* or because of the parallel development of various words with those initial clusters, many later such English words "attracted" the sense of 'chaos, ruin; disorder, dirt, messiness,' to wit: *skimble-skamble, shambles, scum, shit, shabby, scab,* etc. (It is important to note that many words from Scandinavian arrived as loanwords in English spelled with initial *sk-* or *sh-,* depending on their pronunciation of the source language at the time. Thus, *skirt* and *shirt* are ultimately traced to the same Icelandic source, *skyrta,* which denoted a garment like a long shirt of today.) It must be said that while correspondences between a narrow set of meanings and a set of similar sounds can often be found, because of the difficulties encountered in establishing precise etymologies for many words caution should be observed in drawing unwarranted conclusions. Though one should abide by this principle, reasonable conjecture and speculation are not forbidden. In time, it appears that *shamble* became narrowed in meaning to a 'kitchen table,' then a 'table in a butcher's shop' (a sense persisting in some dialects in Britain), and, by association with the general carnage of the slaughterhouse, to 'disarray, disorder, and destruction.' On the way to its 'destruction,' *shambles* paused in the early nineteenth century in America to acquire the sense of a 'slave market,' and an example of that use, which faded, appears in *Uncle Tom's Cabin*. The word is probably applied today more often than not to the condition of a teenager's bedroom.

SHRINK

Most people know this mildly vituperative term for 'psychiatrist' to come from *headshrinker,* but there is a tale that has sprung up, particularly among amateur etymologists, that psychiatrists are so called when their patients visit them because they suffer from inflated egos, the consultant's function being to "cut them down to size." A moment's reflection will confirm the ludicrousness of such a notion: people visit psychiatrists (as well as psychoanalysts, psychologists, lay analysts, etc.) for a great variety of reasons, but in the "ego department" more likely because they feel inferior and lacking in confidence than the opposite: they do not pay all that money to be "whittled (back) down to (their proper) size." The Jivaro headhunters of South America removed the brains of their victims but retained the skin, scalp, and skull intact, filling the cavity with hot sand, which served to shrink a normal skull to the size of a large avocado (for lack of a better image). The witch doctors of the Indian tribes used these shrunken skulls as amulets and as objects of worship, divination, and other ritualistic practices. The adoption of *headshrinker* for 'psychiatrist' had jocular, sardonic beginnings, meaning something like 'witch doctor' but with overtones that reflected the underlying resentment that patients occasionally feel over the fees they must pay.

SKID ROW

It is not easy to see why, but Seattle swells with pride in the well-documented knowledge that *skid row* had its origins there. In the mid nineteenth century a logging road along which logs were skidded (*Skid Road*) led from the place where loggers hauled trees from the forest to Yesler's Mill, at the foot of an incline. It is understandable that such a thoroughfare would scarcely become the focus of the better commercial establishments or be as attractive as a residential neighborhood. In fact, it became a road populated by lumberjacks, sailors, and the rough trade that frequently accompanies them—prostitutes, panhandlers, bunco artists (see **bunk**), and so on. The name *Skid Road* metamorphosed into *Skid Row,* which by the end of the century had become the figurative name for any city street and its neighborhood blighted by vagrants, tramps, alcoholics, and other pariahs. It is today always spelled with small letters.

SKIN FLICK

This slang term originated in the mid twentieth century, and refers to a pornographic, X-rated movie, though the reference is to the nudity of the performers. After its enormous popularity in the early 1980s, the television film *Roots* was referred to as a "kin flick."

SLEEVELESS ERRAND

This ancient expression—quotations from the earliest English writings appear in the *OED*—is commonly thought to have come from *sleave* 'knotted ends of a piece of woven fabric'; hence, the story goes, a *sleeveless* (or *sleaveless*) *errand* is one in which these ends are not knotted but loose, thus making the person who performs it "at loose ends." The only fault with this etymology is that examples of the phrase with the spelling *sleaveless* are not found; besides, the sense 'at loose ends' cannot be said to be the same as 'without aim or purpose,' the sense of *sleeveless* in the idiom. It seems far more likely that another sense of *sleeve* was used, namely, for a 'token of a lady's favor often worn by knights errant,' for which citations abound. Thus, a *sleeveless errand* was simply one without a sponsor, or purpose, which is much closer to the more modern sense. In some modern contexts, *sleeveless errand* has been used to refer to the sort of practical joke played on a novice when he is sent in search of a bucket of steam, a left-handed monkeywrench, or a can of striped paint.

SMOKEY (THE) BEAR

This term became a nickname—originally a code word—among citizen's band radio operators on the U.S. highways for a 'state policeman.' Word archaeologists of the twenty-fifth century will muse over the etymology of this name and it is anybody's guess what sort of imaginative creations they will produce without the real facts. The facts for contemporaries are simple: *Smokey the Bear,* an upright-standing brown bear wearing a military hat that was left over from the period between the world wars—at least, the last time it seems to have been used in the U.S. Army it appears in motion pictures set at the beginning of World War II, usually at Pearl Harbor, Hawaii—was created as a symbol for posters and other media by the U.S. Forestry Service. Smokey's main function is to warn people, "Only *you* can prevent forest fires!" For some reason, the broad-brimmed military hat with the high crown bearing dents at the four points of the compass was adopted as part of the uniform by a number of state police units throughout the United States (though many wear a hat that more closely resembles a homburg). *Smokey* and *Smokey Bear* became names by which CB'ers identified the state police patrols, especially in warning other drivers of their presence, thus allowing them to reduce their speed to something within the range of the posted limit.

SNEAKY PETE

'Cheap muscatel wine laced with a narcotic,' often used by winos for an extra kick. Also called *Sweet Lucy, smoke.*

SOMETHING ON A STICK

An Ozark expression for 'something special': *She really thinks he's something on a stick.* The origin can probably be traced to a "treat," like a chocolate-covered ice cream on a stick.

SON-OF-A-BITCH STEW

Unlikely to be found on the menus of four-star restaurants, this dish was said to have been common (if not exactly popular) as chuck-wagon fare in the Old West; the only star it might have been associated with was the one in the flag of Texas. Hendrickson describes this as a stew made from offal—the entrails of a steer (though a bull or cow would probably have served as well)—and the "indispensable ingredient was guts (tripe)." According to Hendrickson, "This inspired the old saying, 'A son of a bitch might not have any brains and no heart, but if he ain't got guts he ain't a son of a bitch.' "

SON OF A SEA-COOK
The food aboard freighters and other merchant vessels was formerly notoriously bad, and, naturally, it was the cook who took the blame. Besides, cooking was woman's work, and the shipboard cook was compelled to suffer the further ignominy of being suspected of being homosexual. Being a sea-cook was thus bad enough; the *son of a sea-cook* was counted among the impossibly lowest of all human beings— so low as not to exist at all—but was used facetiously more often than seriously.

SOUND AS A BELL
An old expression in which sound has its usual meaning of 'very well, very good,' often 'quite healthy.' Although the simile comes from the notion that a bell must have no crack in order to ring true, it is also a play on words: "to sound as a bell sounds." The phrase goes back to the sixteenth century and appears in Shakespeare's *Much Ado About Nothing*.

SPEND A PENNY
Britain, not being an underprivileged country, once had pay toilets, as did America, though the fee was a penny, not, as in America, a nickel or a dime. Although financial exploitation of the incontinent seems to have disappeared from both continents, *spend a penny* remains a British euphemism otherwise expressed, especially in the U.S., as *go to the little boys'* (or *girls'*) *room, go to the bathroom, wash one's hands,* etc. It is said that the limbo, the Caribbean

dance in which a performer, still on his feet, moves crab-like beneath an ever-lowered horizontal stick to the rhythms of a steel band, originated in Scotland when pay toilets were first installed. A true anecdote is told about an American businessman who urged that it would be advantageous to increase the advertising budget for a product to be marketed by a British company. He tried to persuade the company's executives of the wisdom of his argument by using a metaphor, "If you want to earn a penny, you've got to spend a penny." Much to his astonishment, the meeting broke up with hilarious laughter.

SPITTIN' IMAGE

The above is a common way of spelling this common idiom, but it also appears as *spit and image, spitting image, spit 'n' image,* and in various other, less frequently encountered forms. Its meaning is 'carbon copy' and it is used in contexts like "She's the spittin' image of ———" (you fill in the blank). The *OED* cites a quotation from 1859 in which *spit and fetch* appears; later citations show *image*. The *Century Dictionary* carries an undated quotation (from the mid nineteenth century) showing the use of *spit* alone, in the sense of 'image, likeness': ". . . a dog. . . . The very spit of the one I had for years." It would seem that in its earlier uses, *spit* in this sense carried the notion of something like 'identical even down to the spit.' It is possible that as the originally obvious meaning of this somewhat abbreviated use became obscure, it was reinforced by . . . *and image.* Recently, commentators have suggested that *spit* is a shortening of *spirit* (becoming *spi'it*), especially as pronounced in the speech of American blacks, yielding the idea that the two things, people, etc., being compared are alike "both in spirit and image (appearance)." There are at least two fallacies in this argument: first, the available citations indicate that the expression was first used in British English, with evidence that it was originally dialectal; second, there is no example known in which the idiom refers to anything more than physical resemblance, and the "spirit" aspect seems to be absent entirely. Such expressions do change, of course, but there has not yet appeared any quotation that would support the "spiritual" theory. The phrase has remained slang or, at best, colloquial (or dialectal), probably because the word *spit* itself (and *spitting*, in particular) have not been admitted to the mincing habits of polite and formal language.

SPLICE THE MAINBRACE

Those who offer an etymology for this nautical idiom, which means to 'partake of grog (or some other alcoholic drink),' suggest that *splicing the mainbrace,* literally, is 'splicing a (presumably) heavy cable used to steady and control the mainyard of a sailing vessel.' Apparently this was a laborious or difficult task for which sailors were customarily issued an extra tot of grog. The evidence confuting this is simple: the term *mainbrace* has been in (written) evidence since the fifteenth century, while *splice the mainbrace* is unattested before the beginning of the nineteenth century; the mainbrace was not necessarily more difficult to splice than any other large brace on a sailing vessel; and the action of splicing is not in any way akin to that of partaking of a ration of grog, nor is the notion of any "extra" issue set forth in *splice the mainbrace.* (*Grog,* incidentally, can be dated to 1740, when Admiral Vernon, nicknamed "Old Grog" because he wore a *grogram,* or *grosgrain* cloak, issued an order allowing British seamen a ration of watered rum.) This somewhat convoluted argument for the origin of *splice the mainbrace* yields to a much simpler explanation: spirituous beverages were long referred to as *bracers,* and it seems far more likely that the issue of grog at the end of the day's work was regarded as the "main bracer." It is here suggested, therefore, that *splice the mainbrace* arose as a jocular nautical reference playing on *mainbrace/main bracer* with *splice* added for nautical spice. It must be added that wordplay was—and is—quite common; the activity of *splicing the mainbrace,* for instance, often took place when *the sun was over the yardarm,* a facetious reference meaning (virtually) "any time of the day at all," as it depends on the point of view of the observer.

STAND THE GAFF

This is a fairly recent Americanism according to the *OED*, which gives 1899 as the date of its earliest citation. Although there is no dispute regarding the modern meaning—'submit to (verbal) abuse'—the earlier sense, 'submit without complaint to blame,' may be fading today. Some sources see a possible connection between this *gaff* and the *gaff* meaning 'spurs of a fighting cock.' Were there no closer, more obvious connection, such an etymology might not be unreasonable. Some even go so far as to see a relationship between *stand the gaff* and *standing gaff*, a nautical term for a 'rig that might lead to some difficulty in handling,' as it refers to a loose-footed gaffsail that is set on a fixed gaff boom. There is no justification in etymological theorizing to cleave to an origin that is labored and obscure (unless all else fails), and in this case there is good evidence for a straightforward link with French *gaffe*, borrowed into English in its original sense of 'blunder,' or, as the *OED* has it, "a remark by which one 'puts one's foot into it,' " its customary modern usage. (*Blow the gaff* means to 'let the cat out of the bag, reveal a plot, or provide convicting evidence,' though this mainly British idiom is traceable to another *gaff*, apparently a variant of *gab*, and seems to have nothing in common with *stand the gaff*.) *Gaff* by itself had a meaning similar to that of modern American English *guff* 'stuff and nonsense, balderdash, humbug; verbal abuse' and *stand the gaff* simply uses *stand* in the common sense of 'abide, tolerate.'

STARK NAKED

An ancient phrase dating from the early sixteenth century according to evidence in the *OED*. Curiously, owing to an apparent misprint in the *Century Dictionary*, twentieth-century observers have etymologized *stark* as *start*, as if "start naked" originally meant 'tail-naked,' in which *start* is taken for earlier *stert* 'tail' (which appears in that sense in *redstart*) or 'naked, the way we start in this world.' This is insupportable, as examination of the citations would immediately reveal: the only place where "start naked" appears is in a cross reference under *stark naked* in the *Century Dictionary*. There is no entry for "start-naked" in that dictionary; the only entry is *stark naked,* listed under the adverbial senses for *stark* along with *stark dead, stark blind, stark drunk,* and *stark mad,* "rarely with other adjectives." In other words, there is no evidence whatsoever for the form "start naked," and it seems curious that earlier investigators would not only have failed to pick up the error but would have accepted it as gospel.

Scribal errors do, of course, occur in language, a typical example being *wolf:* there is no other explanation for pronouncing this word as if it were spelled "wulf"; indeed, it is pronounced "wolf" in other Indo-European languages. A scribal oddment is the spelling form of *Do's and Don'ts,* where, for consistency, the phrase should be spelled either *Dos and Don'ts* or *Do's and Don't's:* evidently, the former yields "Dos," a nonstarter as an English word, while the latter yields "Don't's," which has too many apostrophes for comfort.

STEAL (SOMEONE'S) THUNDER

The story of the source of this expression, which means to 'usurp from its rightful proprietor the credit for an original act, action, idea, invention, discovery, etc., and the glory that goes with it,' is outlandish enough to be believable. It is said that a playwright, John Dennis (1657–1734) invented a means for reproducing on stage a sound effect resembling thunder, which he used in one of his (unsuccessful) plays. Later on, the device was imitated by another in a production of *Macbeth,* whereupon Dennis was recorded as saying, with appropriate indignation, that this parvenu had *stolen his thunder.* Like many stories, this one supplies a logical trace to the beginnings of a phrase; whether it is true or not seems less important.

STIFF (A WAITER)

To *stiff a waiter* means to 'leave no tip,' and a nontipper is called a *stiff. Bindle stiff* is a 'tramp (who carries his belongings in a bindle, variant of *bundle*).' These senses of *stiff* probably have their origins in *stiff man,* a lowly employee on a Western ranch with the responsibility of disposing of corpses, or *stiffs,* by burning them. Such people were regarded as being worthless, and *stiff* evolved as a pejorative term for such a person, later becoming more generalized into two applications: a designation similar to guy or fellow but with the critical overtones of a 'sucker, someone who is being taken advantage of,' as in *working stiff;* in an even less complimentary context, a 'square, someone who is out of it.' Restaurant employees could scarcely hold nontippers in high regard, hence the designation and the resultant verb, to *stiff.*

STIR-CRAZY

Stir is criminal slang for 'prison,' a metaphor that might, at first glance, seem to have been born of the image of one's movements being limited to a small confined area. In fact, though, *stir* goes back to the Old English word *steor* 'imprisonment, confinement,' which, as far as is known, survives only in this relic. Prisoners who become neurotic or psychotic from such confinement are termed *stir-crazy* if their behavior is regarded as irrational. In any event, incarceration is scarcely a stirring experience.

STOOL PIGEON

This is a well-documented American metaphor of the nineteenth century according to most sources; but its origins lie in fifteenth-century English and can be traced to thirteenth-century French. The earliest senses appear in the form *stale,* judged as coming from Anglo-French (thirteenth century) *estale,* or *estal,* which later occurs in continental French as *estalon,* all with the meaning 'decoy bird, a living bird used to entice other birds of its own species, or birds of prey, into a snare or net'; figuratively, a 'lure.' In this form, the word appears in the sixteenth century in the sense of a 'thief's accomplice.' The *OED* offers the word as of Germanic origin, appearing as *stellvogel,* Modern German *Lockvogel,* with the same meaning. A later variant, *stall,* is attested for 'decoy bird' in the sixteenth century, when the sense of a 'pickpocket's accomplice who diverts the attention of a victim' is strengthened and continues to modern times. At that time, the verb *stall* also came into use, originally with the connotation of 'deception'; only latterly did the simple notion of 'delay' become associated with *stall*. As we use it today, *stall* in *stall for time* carries along the suggestion that the real reason for delay is not being made apparent, but outright dishonesty is not necessarily implied. The shift to *stool,* which has been found only in American English dating from the mid nineteenth century, was accompanied by a concentration (once again) on the literal meaning, 'decoy bird.' It seems likely that the 'stool' sense was reinforced by the perch on which the live decoy was placed, for by that time, *stale* in its older sense was obsolete and *stall* had become specialized in its sense of 'delay.' In its later incarnations, evidently because the *stool* was itself almost invariably a pigeon, the term *stool pigeon* came into use in American English and quickly acquired a specialized figurative use among gamblers as 'decoy.' Another function of these accomplices must have been to stand behind a card-player's chair and signal his holding to a confederate, thus giving rise to the modern sense of 'one who betrays a confidence,' especially 'one who informs to the police.' In Modern English, *stool pigeon* has been shortened to *stoolie* and, by transference (through the fanciful notion that even such "birds" sing), to *canary*. The other part of the modern term, *pigeon,* in the sense of 'sucker, dupe, victim of a swindle,' has a collateral history in English, going back to the sixteenth century, supported by the harmless nature of that bird and the ease with which it is caught. The same use of *pigeon* occurs in Modern French, which also has *pigeonner* to 'dupe, swindle.' These words in all of their modern uses are slang.

STRAWBERRY FRIEND
An Ozark epithet for a 'sponger, freeloader, moocher,' that is, someone, as from the city, who visits only when the strawberries are ready for picking.

STRAWHAT CIRCUIT
In the 1930s, when many Broadway theaters closed for the summer, there sprang up outside of New York City a number of local playhouses that catered to the entertainment needs of those who sojourned in the country. This provided the visitors as well as the indigenous population with the opportunity to enjoy the older Broadway shows without traveling very far. The actors were, of course, only too happy to be working, even if the staging, often in a converted barn or town hall, was somewhat primitive compared with the Big Time of New York. Gradually, the theaters became more permanently established and better equipped, attracting top Broadway stars, producers, and directors. Local hopefuls filled in the lesser roles. The Westport Country Playhouse, in Westport, Connecticut, was for many years owned and operated by the Theatre Guild, under the direction of Lawrence Langner and Theresa Helburn, and it became quite famous—especially after the Guild's *Oklahoma!* became a smash hit on Broadway. The entire cycle of bookings, which later led to the scheduling of about nine plays, staged sequentially by the same company in one summer stock theater after another during July and August, came to be called the *strawhat circuit* after its bucolic beginnings. See also **borscht belt** or **circuit**.

STREET SMARTS
This is a phrase that has come into the American language since the 1960s to designate a 'measure of clever sophistication based on experience gained from frequenting the streets of a large city and associating with the people who spend their time there'—usually dope peddlers, gamblers,

bookies, pimps, prostitutes, grifters and drifters, vagrants, and others who are regarded as wise in the ways of the world. The person who has *street smarts* is *streetwise*. These terms are applied in a complimentary manner to adult males, teenagers, or even children, rarely to women.

STRING (SOMEONE) ALONG

In the sense of 'fool, deceive,' this verb phrase appeared rather recently in the language, but its origins are quite ancient. The noun *string,* as will be readily acknowledged, has a great number of metaphoric possibilities. A seventeenth- or eighteenth-century expression, to *have in* (or *on*) *a string* meant to 'have under control, be able to do what one likes with' (*OED*). This was later reinforced by to *have on a string,* in reference to "control of someone as if he were a puppet on a string." The *Century Dictionary* lists the sense 'hoax or discredited story,' labeling it "Printers' slang, England," but this is not found in the *OED*. In any event, *string,* also used in the sense of 'trap, snare,' lends itself readily to such extensions, and *string along* would appear to be a modern reinforced verbal version of the older transferred meaning of the noun. The earliest citations for *string along* are dated 1901 and 1910.

T

TAKE A (RUNOUT) POWDER

This slang verb phrase, with or without the embellishing *runout,* means to 'depart hurriedly; take it on the lam.' The *OED* lists noun and verb entries for *powder* that, because of the differences in meaning, are not from the same source as *powder* meaning a 'comminuted, or pulverized substance' or, as a verb, to 'make into a powder.' This other *powder* means an 'impetus, rush; force, impetuosity' or (as a verb) to 'rush; hurry with impetuosity and rushing speed; said of a rider.' The senses do not appear quite so remote from one another if one considers two meanings of *powder* (the noun, from which the verb is taken): one is the word for a *magical powder,* one used by sorcerers—perhaps to make someone invisible. (Perhaps, as in the case of *gunpowder,* to make someone disappear?) The other could have the meaning of 'reduce to such insignificance as to be readily blown away.' As can be seen, the sense 'decamp precipitately' is present in the word and has been sustained since the early seventeenth century.

TAKE A SHINE TO (SOMEONE or SOMETHING)

In the idiomatic sense 'take a liking to,' the origin of this expression is obscure. The *Century Dictionary* labels it "Low, U.S.," the *OED* merely "U.S." The *OED* also suggests that it may have nothing to do with *shine* 'send forth or reflect brilliance,' yet may possibly be related to another *shine,* a dialectal variant of *shindy,* though the semantic connection to that word seems tenuous. *Shindy* is itself of doubtful origin, possibly from *shinty,* a 'kind of ballgame' according to the *OED.* Though *shindig* in most dictionaries is given as a variant of *shinny, shindy,* or *shinty,* it may well be the basic word: perhaps it is just what it sounds like, *shin + dig,* that is, some activity in which the *shins* must endure some *digging,* like (field) hockey or a wild dance or even a brawl. If such is the case, then the *shine* of *take a shine to* would probably be unrelated. Rather, it may come from the verb phrase *shine up to* 'endear or ingratiate oneself to,' that is, to 'make oneself "shining" (i.e., desirable) in the eyes of.' Conversion of the verb phrase might well have yielded *take a shine to,* but evidence is lacking. In any event, it is an Americanism dating from the early nineteenth century.

TAKE FOR A RIDE
There are two different senses for this idiom. One, meaning to 'cheat, cozen, dupe,' comes from the metaphorical meaning to 'dominate, tease' for *ride* perhaps influenced by *deride* 'make ridiculous.' The other, also a recent use and American in origin, means to 'murder.' There is no evidence for its existence before the use of cars, and it refers jocularly to *ride* in the sense of an 'excursion,' though one from which the victim does not return. The citations for this usage are entirely from fictional sources, and it is impossible to say whether it had any currency among criminals before its appearance in gangster movies or whodunits.

TAKE THE CAKE
This apparently transparent expression does, indeed, mean 'win the prize or the honors.' But its specific origins are tied to the dance called the *cakewalk,* a nineteenth-century competition, usually confined to black participants, in which those couples who performed best and were decked out in the most decorative way won the prize—a *cake.*

TALKING HEAD

A 'person on television who holds forth' on any subject—as contrasted with someone whose purpose it is to amuse or entertain. The latest manifestation, the ultimate in talking heads is Max Headroom, a character synthetically produced by computer electronics. Though not, strictly speaking, totally devoid of entertainment value, Max Headroom is essentially a satire on *talking heads*.

TALK THROUGH ONE'S HAT

The traditional sources give the origin of this expression, which means to 'bluster; say things with no authority; fictionalize,' as coming from the more or less physical notion of one's talking "over one's head." That is a reasonable enough guess, but it might be interesting to suggest another: perhaps the blowhard in question used a megaphone to trumpet forth his self-serving promotion; a megaphone worn on the head resembles, suitably, a dunce-cap. Thus, such a paragon of pomposity could "literally" be said to be *talking through his hat*. Variants are to *talk off the top of one's head* (which can also mean 'talk extemporaneously'), *talk through the back of one's neck, talk big*—and there are sure to be others.

TAXI DANCER

A 'woman who works in a dance-hall, dancing with partners in exchange for tickets that they purchase at the door.' The dancer cashes in the tickets she collects and is paid a percentage of the price paid for them. She is called a *taxi dancer* because she goes from one partner to another, at the beck and call of the customer. There is an old song, part of which goes:

. . . And as a dollar goes from hand to hand,
A woman goes from man to man
—In a taxi—
A woman goes from man to man.

TEACH ONE'S GRANDMOTHER HOW TO SUCK EGGS

This cliché means '(be so presumptuous as to) give advice to one's elders or to someone who is an acknowledged authority on a subject.' It has been around for centuries; an earlier version of it was *teach one's (gran)dame to spin*. What is so curious about the expression is that it is so archaically rustic-sounding: people who first hear it are given to wonder about all this egg-sucking that is going on at granny's, for they have never seen or experienced it. It may be conjectured that in these enlightened times, when the availability of false teeth enables grannies to eat steak, their diet is no longer restricted to milktoast, sour milk, and raw eggs.

TEAR THE BONE OUT

An Ozark phrase meaning to 'let go, go the whole hog, engage in energetically, pull out all the stops.'

TEE OFF ON SOMEONE

Tee off is from golf, but there is no semantic connection between golf and the meaning of this phrase. In the form *tee off on someone* it means 'suddenly vent one's anger at someone'; in the form *teed off* it means 'angry, annoyed, vexed.' It seems likely that the second gave rise to the first, and *teed off* is probably a change from *peed off* which is a (baby-talk) euphemism for *pissed off,* which means the same thing. Changing *teed off* from a passive to an active verb yields *tee off on* (or *against*). On the other hand, *tee off on* may be a loan idiom from British English *tick off* 'reprimand,' in which *tick* is equivalent to American *check*—the kind of mark one would make against another's name in a list of items: failure to come up to standard would result in a reproof in which the subordinate would become *ticked off* 'annoyed' at his superior's having *ticked him off* 'rebuked him.'

TENDERLOIN

This term provides an excellent example of how interpretations of a metaphor's possible origin can differ. The earliest use of the word is reasonably well documented in a report by a New York City police lieutenant named Williams, in which the West Side of Manhattan between Twenty-third and Forty-second streets was referred to as the *tenderloin* because of all of the crime and graft. Some observers believe that the name arose because the police benefited from graft to such an extent that they could afford to eat tenderloin, a very expensive cut of beef, rather than potatoes and boiled cabbage. It seems equally likely, though, that the name was applied to that section of the city which, like the *tenderloin* of the steer, was small, select, and very, very rich and exclusive—ripe for graft.

THAT'S THE WAY THE COOKIE CRUMBLES

This cliché and others like it appeared in the 1950s and, according to some, originated on Mad(ison) Avenue. Uttered in response or complementation to some expressed lament—"My dog was killed in the sausage machine yesterday," "I lost my contact lens in their swimming pool," and other cataclysms—the pattern of alliteration became a word game to avoid the boring repetition of the original: *That's the way the ball bounces, the matzoh meals, the mop flops, the water works,* etc., ad nauseam.

THE DEVIL TO PAY (AND NO PITCH HOT)

The argument against *devil* in the sense 'seam at the garboard strake' is set forth under **between the devil and the deep blue sea** and will not be repeated here. *Pay* in the nautical sense, 'fill a seam,' is well attested. Among folk etymologists, *the devil to pay* is greeted with inordinate delight because it yields what they regard as further affirmation of *devil* 'seam,' but there is no more justification for that meaning in this context than in any other. The *Century Dictionary* supports the "seam" theory but suggests that the seam in question is at the waterline. This is not easily acceptable both because waterline seams seldom give trouble and because their repair is usually accomplished (in calm waters) rather easily, merely by careening the boat slightly. The *Century* also defines the expression as meaning "great mischief afoot; riotous disturbance; any serious and especially unexpected difficulty or entanglement; a difficulty to be overcome," which is at variance with the meanings documented elsewhere. *The devil to pay* most likely meant just that originally: 'one must accept the responsibility for the consequences of his (evil) actions.' *Pay* in the sense 'fill a seam' yielded the possibility for a play on words, to which *and no pitch hot* was added for reinforcement, hot pitch having been poured into seams to make them watertight by sealing the oakum caulking. Sadly, a piece in *The New York Times Magazine* (March 22, 1987) seeks to perpetuate the old etymologies for *the devil to pay* and *between the devil and the deep blue sea;* its author even embellishes the fanciful tale by identifying the *devil* as "the longest seam—just below the main deck, between two planks on the vessel's hull—running from stem to stern without a break." This is patent nonsense to anyone familiar with wooden vessel construction, for all seams in such a hull run "from stem to stern without a break." *Pay* in the ship maintenance sense has the past *payed*, not *paid*.

THE $64 QUESTION

This Americanism, which has achieved worldwide acceptance, started in 1940 with a radio quiz show, *Double or Nothing*. Beginning with one dollar, a contestant was asked a question on a subject chosen by him from a list provided; if he answered correctly, he received two dollars and was given the choice of taking the money or doubling it by correctly answering another question. The doubling continued as did the difficulty of the questions, the hardest being the last one, the correct answer to which doubled the prize money from $32 to $64. It was called *the $64 question,* and the phrase caught on, being used to mean 'the critical, key, most difficult question.' Inflation being what it is, when the show was revived for television in the 1950s, the prize money was increased by a factor of one thousand, with the grand prize at $64,000 and the contestant enclosed in an "isolation booth," both for dramatic effect and to prevent prompting from the audience. The title of this show was *The $64,000 Question.* Since that time *$64,000 question* has been heard a bit more frequently than *$64 Question.* The television show disappeared in a cloud of ignominy when it was revealed that its producers had provided some of the contestants with the answers in advance.

THERE'S THE RUB
The noun *rub* dates as early as the sixteenth century in the sense of an 'impediment, obstacle,' especially applied to some sort of hindrance encountered in the game of bowls, and there are many citations for its use. The figurative application in Shakespeare, "To sleep, perchance to dream: ay, there's the rub," (*Hamlet,* III, i, 65) was common at the time and, reinforced by this use in Hamlet's soliloquy, remains well known today.

THIRD WORLD
This rather depreciatory, derogatory, supercilious, insulting epithet was coined in the 1950s or '60s to describe those countries of the world that were otherwise called "developing," a euphemism for "undeveloped" or "underdeveloped." The hierarchy—apparently—had the United States, Britain, other western European nations, the Soviet Union, and a handful of other countries—Japan, Australia, etc.—as making up the theoretical "First World," though that was never mentioned. Referred to only obliquely and by suggestion, were countries like those in Central and South America, which were inhabited mainly by descendants of Europeans: these constituted the unmentionable "Second World." The *Third World* consisted—consists—

of those countries that (1) gained independence from their former status as colonies of European regimes; (2) are inhabited mainly by blacks; (3) have little or no industry; (4) are often in a state of political upheaval (some of it brought about by the insidious imperialism of "First" or "Second World" nations; and (5) have natural resources that are of great importance to the so-called "developed" nations that try to exploit them.

THREE-DOG NIGHT
As the common folklore would have it, those who survive in the far north—Alaska, the Yukon, and so forth—are wont to bed down with their sled dogs for warmth. Thus, a *three-* or, possibly, a *four-dog night* is just that much colder than a *one-* or *two-dog night*. The expression is of relatively recent origin, some say from the Eskimos.

THREE SHEETS TO THE WIND
In nautical parlance, a *sheet* is a line (the landlubber's "rope") attached to the corner of a sail or to the end of a wooden spar (or boom) to which a sail is attached in order to control its position relative to the wind. In a strong wind, if the end of the sheet is let go, it may be carried overboard or stretched out like a streamer in the breeze, making it difficult to recover. In the meanwhile, the sail flaps crazily (and, often, dangerously) in the wind, and the vessel is difficult or even impossible to control, pitching and yawing this way and that. The image of a boat has been likened to the movements of a wildly careening, drunken sailor, staggering down the street, unable to control his legs, and any tipsy toper is today said to be *three sheets to the wind*.

THROW COLD WATER ON (SOMETHING)

The "something" is usually any activity and the entire expression means to 'put a damper on something, discourage the consideration of a plan, etc.' (in which *damper* is the choking device in a chimney, not a wetting agent). Although other commentators have suggested that the phrase originated from the literal sense of 'shock by administering a cold shower-bath,' it is a more interesting—and no less likely—conjecture that the literal action was to follow the practice of those who would stop a pair of dogs from mating (as in the street) by throwing cold water on them. This activity has been engaged in far more often in connection with dogs than with people, notwithstanding the puritanical backgrounds of the earlier inhabitants of New England. It has a telling effect on cooling the ardor of the participants, as may be imagined.

THROWN FOR A LOSS

An idiom from American football in which a team in possession of the ball loses ground by being caught with the ball in its backfield, behind the line of scrimmage, thus "advancing backward." *Lose ground* is probably a military metaphor, and not from sports.

THROW OUT THE BABY WITH THE BATHWATER

This expression, suggesting that one is going a bit too far in whatever one is doing, is probably British in origin. Partridge traces it back to the mid 1940s and calls into consideration "the German proverbial *Das Kind mit dem Bade ausgiessen*."

TIN PAN ALLEY

This is the metaphoric name given to the popular-music business in general, and not to a specific place. In the past, commentators have tried to associate it with a particular site, like the Brill Building, in New York City, where many music publishers once had their offices. There were a number of music publishers' offices on East Twenty-eighth Street in the 1920s, and the name might have originated with them. But even in those days Tin Pan Alley referred generically to the business and no particular area or place. Today, with popular-music publishers situated all over the United States, such attempts at localization make even less sense. The term is used in England with the same meaning, and the area designated has traditionally been the Charing Cross section of London.

TOADY

This is a common synonym for 'obsequious flatterer, sycophant, apple polisher, brown-noser, bootlicker, lick-spittle'—the list is long enough to make one wonder if the profusion of such low types is in proportion to their share of the lexicon. *Toady* is short for *toad-eater,* the name given to a professional charlatan's assistant who pretended to swallow (or might actually have swallowed) supposedly poisonous toads in order to demonstrate the lifesaving qualities of his employer's quack remedies: since snakes are known to destroy frogs and toads, perhaps it was snake oil. The transference of this literal use to the figurative is captured in a rare explanation of such phenomena in Sarah Fielding's *David Simple* (1744–52):

> It is a Metaphor taken from a Mountebank's Boy's eating Toads, in order to show his Master's Skill in expelling Poison. It is built on Supposition that People who are in a State of Dependance, are forced to do the most nauseous things that can be thought on, to please and humor their Patrons.

The shortening from *toad-eater* to *toady* does not seem to have diminished the fervor with which such grovelers behave nor, indeed, their number. *Brown-noser,* from the verb *brown-nose,* is a synonym that had vulgar origins; because it sounds harmless enough, many do not suspect that it comes from naming the posture of one whose nose is stuck firmly up another's rear end in abject subservience.

TO THE MANNER BORN

An old British expression, now universal in English, that in Shakespearian use meant 'familiar with (a particular practice) because of long experience, as from birth.' It has lately taken on a somewhat more elevated sense, implying high birth and good breeding, probably because *manner* is sometimes taken to be *manor*.

TOUCH AND GO

This expression, which today means 'iffy, precarious' more often than its earlier sense of 'quick movement,' has a nautical origin: when a vessel is in relatively shallow waters so that its bottom occasionally touches the ground beneath but then moves off without damage, that situation is called *touch and go* (literally). See also **hard and fast.**

TURN THE TABLES

Those few sources that offer comment on this expression— including the *OED*—trace it to the turning about the gaming table so that a player is playing with the cards, men, or other implements of the game that were formerly held by his adversary, and vice versa. Although this is a very neat explanation, it does not make much sense, and there are no games that can be found in which such a maneuver is performed—at least, not according to the rules. In backgammon, however, the game itself was once called *tables,* and the two halves of the playing board are still called *tables.* In the complex rules of the game, which will not be described here, each player's object, having made a circuit of the board, is to bring his men into his own inner *table,* whereupon the men are "borne off" to conclude the game. If in the course of play, according to Captain Rawley's *Handy Book of Games for Gentlemen* (London, 1868), "When running to avoid a gammon, and having two men on the enemy's ace point, move any of their fellows rather than them. . . . [Y]our opponent may be compelled to leave blots which you may hit once—yea, twice—and the tables may be turned." The sense, associated with conquest, is that the player has changed a (possibly) losing situation into a winning one. The Theories abound as to the origin of backgammon itself—vestiges of similar games have been discovered among the artifacts of the ancient Greek, Japanese, and Egyptian civilizations, and an illustration of a backgammon-like game appears in the Harleian manuscript collection. The rules of *tables,* the earlier name for the game, appear in a fourteenth-century manuscript, and decrees issued by Richard the Lionhearted forbade the playing at backgammon for money by any military man under the rank of knight. The game was universally popular throughout Europe, known in Italy as *tavola reale* 'royal table.' As *tables* it appears in *Love's Labour's Lost* (V,ii,328) and, indeed, in earlier sources. The phrase appears in the passive as *the tables are* (or *have been*) *turned.*

U

UNCLE TOM, UNCLE TOMISM

Uncle Tom's Cabin (1852), by Harriet Beecher Stowe, was
an antislavery novel that had incredibly great impact in
America and elsewhere as a dramatization of the plight of
black slaves in the southern states, and it would require
reams merely to document the history of its effects. In it,
Uncle Tom, an elderly black, is portrayed as a servile and
deferential slave on a southern plantation. If a black behaves
in this manner and is—or appears to be—particularly obsequious to a white person, other blacks call him an *Uncle
Tom*, a term of hateful obloquy. *Uncle Tomism*, on the
other hand, describes the principles and practices of a white
supremacist. Both terms are fairly new: the earliest citation
in the *OED* for *Uncle Tom* is dated 1922, that for *Uncle
Tomism*, 1937.

W

WAKE (UP) THE WRONG PASSENGER

This expression, referring to a passenger on public transport, usually a train, can easily be understood in its literal applications. Figuratively, it means to 'misjudge an adversary or the person with whom one has to deal.' Dating from the mid nineteenth century is a revealing quotation (*DAE,* 1856): "It was evident to the Doctor that, in Western parlance, 'he had waked the wrong passenger.' There was to be a struggle [with the rattlesnake]."

WALK SPANISH

From the sixteenth century onward, English-speaking peoples seem to have had problems with those who speak Spanish. The defeat of the Spanish Armada (1588) settled matters for a while in England, but then the Spanish started acting up again in the New World, and the history of Spanish influence in America is not a savory one, from the conquest and destruction of the Aztec, Mayan, and Incan civilizations, to their influence in Mexico against the United States, to their ultimate capitulation in 1898 in the Spanish-

American War. Notwithstanding, this long history of conflict, which might be conceived of as having given rise to some very nasty idiomatic expressions involving Spain and Spaniards in the English language, had no apparent connection with the verb phrase *walk Spanish,* which means to 'walk or cause to walk on tiptoes as when firmly grasped by the scruff of the neck and the seat of the pants, especially while ejecting someone from a place.' In other words, it is what is otherwise known in American slang as the *bum's rush.* The only available theory of its origin conjures up the image of a (male) Spanish flamenco dancer, who characteristically dances on his toes—the way a person who is being *walked Spanish* might do—before stamping down hard on his heels to the accompaniment of suitable music.

The British (at least) have had their problems with the French too; but again, there is no connection between the French and the term *frog-march* 'carry (a person, especially a violent prisoner) facedown, with one man holding each limb.' This is a slight transference from the literal image of the way a frog moves along the ground on its belly, with its four legs splayed outward. It would seem that any earlier prejudices felt by English speakers against the French or Spanish have long since disappeared. Yet, there still lurk in each language some idioms that betoken the older ill feeling: what in English is known as *French leave* is *filer à l'anglaise* in French (and *sich auf französisch empfehlen* in German); *French letter* is *capote anglaise* in French (and *Pariser* in German); *syphilis* was formerly called *the French disease* in England and *la maladie anglaise* in France; and *avoir ses anglais* is French slang for 'to have a menstrual period.' On the other hand, for some unaccountable reason, the innocuous sewing term, *French seam,* is called *couture anglaise* in French; *assiette anglaise* = assorted cold roast meats; *crème anglaise* = egg custard. In Italian, *zuppa inglese* (literally, 'English soup') means a 'trifle.' A term for *rickets* in German is *die englische Krankheit,* and *ein Engländer* is a *monkey wrench* (or *adjustable spanner*); an (archaic) German term for *syphilis* was *die französische Krankheit; that's Greek to me* appears in

German as *das kommt mir spanisch vor;* and *to be very proud* is *stolz wie ein Spanier sein.* The interlingual picture clouds over when one finds that the name for the dog that in American English is called a *German shepherd* (*deutscher Schäferhund*—literally the same thing—in German) is called an *Alsatian* in British English. A full discussion of such national and ethnic identifications is probably best left to an independent study to avoid getting *in Dutch* by exhibiting too much *Dutch courage.*

WALTER MITTY

This eponym for a 'daydreamer, fantasist' is the creation of James Thurber, who wrote "The Secret Life of Walter Mitty," in 1939. It was later made into a popular motion picture that has been widely exhibited, and the term entered the language. In recent years, in England, it has to some extent been replaced by *Billy Liar,* a young man who, like Walter Mitty, succumbs to the vivid fantasies of brave acts, sexual conquests, and the like with which his fertile imagination is beset. Like Mitty, Billy's daydreams more often than not spell trouble for him. Yet, in the end, all turns out for the best for both.

WATCH THE SUBMARINE RACES

This curious Americanism, coined by the New York disk jockey Murray the K in the 1950s, is a cloudy euphemism for 'make out,' a colloquial version of 'engage in sexual dalliance' as the Victorian writers would have it. It referred particularly to the activity characteristic of teenagers in the back seat of a car, especially one parked toward the rear of drive-in movie theaters. Drive-ins have now all but disappeared from the landscape, and modern mores and morals being what they are in the "permissive society," the entire notion of such sport being carried on clandestinely is passé. To be sure, any attempt at giving a literal meaning to the expression from which a metaphorical interpretation might be derivable would prove pointless.

WEASEL WORD
Weasels proverbially suck the insides from eggs, leaving the empty shell. *Weasel words* are empty words, words that sound important but are hollow.

WEDGE-FLOATING
A term used in the Ozarks to mean 'strong, concentrated.' It comes from the test used to check the strength of coffee: an iron wedge is dropped into the coffeepot: if the wedge floats, the coffee may be a wee bit too strong.

WELL-HEELED
It is likely that there are two American idioms at work here. The one meaning 'rich, amply supplied with funds' can be interpreted as having been coined, perhaps facetiously, as the opposite of *down at the heels* 'poor, in reduced circumstances, on one's uppers.' The other, originally just *heeled* 'armed, especially with a pistol,' is traceable to a term used in reference to fighting cocks, which are provided with sharp steel spurs fastened to their legs.

WHAM, BAM, THANK YOU, MA'AM
This modern vulgar American expression (1895) refers to a quick sexual encounter with no emotional involvement, otherwise coarsely called a *quickie*. Although the phrase is used somewhat humorously by men, it is quite justifiably considered denigrating and insulting by women who do not wish to be regarded solely as sexual objects.

WHERE THE SUN DON'T SHINE
There is no purist's version of this (with "doesn't"), any more than one can probably use "isn't" in "The old gray mare, She ain't what she used to be. . . ." This amusing expression refers not to London and its weather but to those parts of the human body that are rarely, if ever, exposed to sunlight, especially outdoors (like the inside of the mouth).

146

WHIPPERSNAPPER

This friendly epithet for a 'young upstart' has a long history in the language, with citations in the *OED* recorded from the seventeenth century. Its etymology is quite transparent—from *whip* + *snapper* 'one who snaps (cracks) whips'—and the *whipper-* is probably from a rhyming duplication of -*snapper* owing to playfulness and euphony. It is always applied to males. From a semantic standpoint, "one who snaps whips" should be viewed as a person who makes some noise but accomplishes little else.

WHIPPING BOY

This is an old term for 'someone who suffers the punishment properly destined for another.' In former times, it was the practice to educate and rear a boy alongside a prince of the royal blood; when the prince misbehaved, because he could not be punished, his *whipping boy* took his place. The only citation (*OED,* 1647) for the literal use of the word may be figurative.

WING IT

Originally theatrical jargon meaning to 'step into a part with little or no preparation,' this common idiom has been extended to include any activity so undertaken. The *OED* suggests that it refers to the hurried study of the role in the wings of the theater; other sources suggest that the reference is to the help given by a prompter who stands in the wings.

WINCHESTER GOOSE

An old slang term for a 'bubo,' that is, a swelling of a lymphatic gland, usually in the groin and usually associated with the (bubonic) plague or with a venereal disease. The term appears in Bacon, Shakespeare, and other writers of the sixteenth and seventeenth centuries. During part of the sixteenth century, the brothels in Southwark, south London, were under the jurisdiction of the Bishop of Winchester, hence the cynical reference.

WOULDN'T TOUCH (SOMETHING) WITH A TEN-FOOT POLE

Sometimes this appears with *barge pole* in place of *ten-foot pole,* but the sentiment remains unchanged. In *American Talk,* Robert Hendrickson suggests that this expression originated in New England, where "boatmen used to pole their boats along in shallow waters." Contrary evidence is not immediately available, but it would seem more likely, in the absence of supportive material from Mr. Hendrickson, that the cliché is southern, where barges and poling were (and still are) more frequently encountered. The author cites *can't touch him with a ten-foot* 'he is distant, proud, reserved' as a Nantucketism from the late nineteenth century.

Y

YABBADABBA DOO!

Today, this has become a cry of exultation, used mainly by children and, according to Partridge, Australian surfers. Its immediate source is the cry uttered in moments of extreme joy by Fred Flintstone, head of the cartoon family depicted in the television series, *The Flintstones,* which portrays a typical American suburban family transported to caveman status (but without the loss of most modern amenities). Nothing, of course, is original, and while *Yabbadabba doo!* is not attested in Neanderthal or even Cro-Magnon speech, it can be traced to an early twentieth-century popular novelty song about chimpanzees and baboons, ending with their going on an "abbadabba honeymoon." (There is no evidence of any connection between the site of that sojourn and the mideastern sheikhdom of Abu Dhabi.)

YELLOW JOURNALISM

The meaning of this pejorative phrase, 'newspaper writing that caters to a low taste for sensationalism,' is only remotely connected with its origin. According to the *OED,* the *New York World* in 1895 published a comic strip "The Yellow Kid," in which the central character was a child dressed in yellow; experimenting with color, the newspaper printed the costume in yellow in an attempt at attracting readers. The first citation for *yellow press* appeared in the (N.Y.) *Daily News* in 1898; *yellow journalism* and other combinations followed soon after. In 1906, the *New*

York Times referred to William Randolph Hearst, the publisher whose newspapers tended toward the sensational, as the " 'yellow' candidate"; *yellowism* appeared in a Springfield, Massachusetts, newspaper in the same year, and the term gained enough currency (and, alas, enough applicability) to remain in the language.

Index

proud, be very **walk Spanish**
quarterback, Monday-morning
 Monday-morning quarterback
quickie **wham, bam, thank you, ma'am**
rack and ruin **hook or by crook, by**
rank and file **grass roots**
rap, beat the **beat the rap**
rap, bum **beat the rap**
rap, take the **beat the rap**
rearing to go **raring to go**
red, paint the town **paint the town red**
rickets **walk Spanish**
ride, take for a **take for a ride**
roaring to go **raring to go**
rock and a hard place, between a **between a rock and a hard place**
roulette, Russian **Russian roulette**
round rimmers **Bowery boy**
rub, there's the **there's the rub**
rubberneck bus **rubberneck**
rubberneck delay **rubberneck**
rubberneck tour **rubberneck**
rustic **cut a rusty**
scamble **shambles, in a**
scarlet creeper **Norfolk Howard**
scribal errors **stark naked**
Scylla and Charybdis, between **between a rock and a hard place**
sea-cook, son of a **son of a sea-cook**
second class **second string**
sell the bearskin . . . **bulls and bears**
set on cinque and sice **at sixes and sevens**
sewing-bee **bee: sewing-bee . . .**
sheet **three sheets to the wind**
sheets to the wind, three **three sheets to the wind**
shindig **take a shine to (someone or something)**
shindy **take a shine to (someone or something)**
shine to, take a **take a shine to (someone or something)**
shine up to **take a shine to (someone or something)**
shinny **take a shine to (someone or something)**
shinty **take a shine to (someone or something)**
shirt **shambles, in a**

sich auf französisch empfehlen **walk Spanish**
single-o cannon **cannon broad**
sink or swim **hook or by crook, by**
sixes and seven, at **at sixes and sevens**
sixty-four-thousand-dollar question **the $64 question**
Skid Road **skid row**
skimble-skamble **shambles, in a**
skirt **shambles, in a**
sleaveless errand **sleeveless errand**
slender, tender, and tall **hook or by crook, by**
smoke **Sneaky Pete**
solo cannon **cannon broad**
soup, in the **in the soup**
Spanish, walk **walk Spanish**
spelling-bee **bee: sewing-bee . . .**
spic and span **hook or by crook, by**
spinning-bee **bee: sewing-bee . . .**
spirit and image **spittin' image**
spit and fetch **spittin' image**
spit and image **spittin' image**
spit 'n' image **spittin' image**
spitting image **spittin' image**
squares **life in the fast lane**
squat **absquatulate**
stall for time **stool-pigeon**
stamping-ground, old **old stamping ground**
standing gaff **stand the gaff**
stark blind **stark naked**
stark dead **stark naked**
stark drunk **stark naked**
stark mad **stark naked**
stew, son of a bitch **son of a bitch stew**
stick, something on a **something on a stick**
stiff man **stiff (a waiter)**
stir **stir-crazy**
stolz wie ein Spanier sein **walk Spanish**
stoolie **stool-pigeon**
stops here, the buck **pass the buck**
streetwise **street smarts**
string, have on a **string (someone) along**
summer cannon **cannon broad**
sun is over the yardarm **splice the mainbrace**
Sweet Lucy **Sneaky Pete**